Unshackled
and FREE

TRUE STORIES OF FORGIVENESS

by CJ & Shelley Hitz

Unshackled & Free
True Stories of Forgiveness

© 2012 by CJ and Shelley Hitz

Printed in the United States of America

Body and Soul Publishing

ISBN-13: 978-0615626376
ISBN-10: 0615626378

Cover design by Megan Six http://msixdesign.com

In Association with The Edge Books

What is THE EDGE?

THE EDGE is a conviction. It's where we stand to save the lost. It's stepping away from our comfortable pews to bring God to the world. It's following Jesus' example to minister to the outcasts, the overlooked, the forgotten.

THE EDGE is about relationship, not religion. It's God's power being stronger and God's love running deeper than anything people face. It's being fearless in the face of adversity and willing to look the devil in the eye and say, "You can't have him or her anymore."

We are authors, Christians, people walking by faith. We are THE EDGE.

www.TheEdgeBooks.blogspot.com

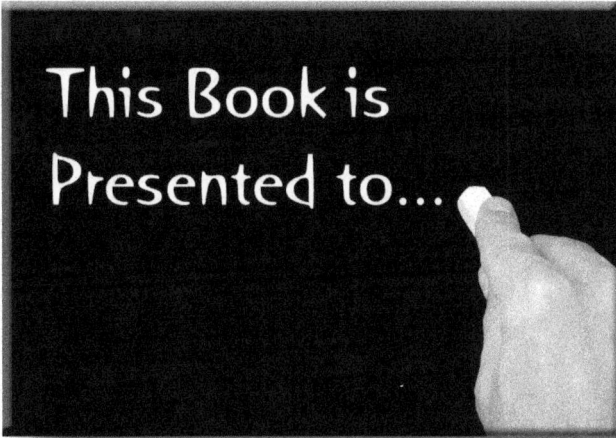

This Book is
Presented to...

To:

From:

Date:

Contents

Introduction

There was once a newspaper that reported the top phrases people love to hear. Number one was "I love you", number two was "dinner is served" and number three was "I forgive you."

Forgiveness. Is. Powerful.

I am passionate about sharing on this topic of forgiveness. Why? Well, just about every major turning point in my life spiritually has started with forgiveness. It's been a powerful catalyst in my life for spiritual growth and healing from wounds of the past.

What Makes Forgiveness So Powerful?

Have you ever been forgiven a debt that you owed to someone else? It feels good to not have to pay that money back, doesn't it? Now, imagine that someone came to you today and said that mortgage, school loans and/or credit card debt has been forgiven. It has been erased and you no longer have to pay those bills. Would you be happy? You bet! Personally, I would be throwing a big party if my mortgage was paid off today.

And so we see that forgiveness is powerful.

The Weight of Unforgiveness

I heard an illustration once about unforgiveness that I will never forget. Imagine that unforgiveness is like carrying a dead corpse around on your back, "piggy back". You carry that weight around everywhere you go.

Do you know what would happen to you physically from carrying a dead person around on your back? It's pretty gross, actually. As the dead corpse continues to rot and decay, it would eventually cause your healthy tissue to rot and decay as well. Over time, it would literally begin to "eat away" at you.

And that's the picture of unforgiveness. Over time, unforgiveness, bitterness and resentment will begin to eat away at us emotionally and spiritually.

And the longer you carry it, the heavier it becomes. Just like carrying a backpack around with you on a long hike that gets heavier with each mile you walk, unforgiveness becomes a heavy weight emotionally and spiritually with each passing day.

What Does the Bible Say About Unforgiveness?

I don't want to assume that you know what the Bible says about unforgiveness, so let's look at a couple verses.

Matthew 6:14-15 says *"For if you forgive men when they sin against you, your heavenly Father will also forgive you. But if you do not forgive men their sins, your Father will not forgive your sins."*

Mark 11:25-26 (AMP) says *"If you have anything against anyone, forgive him and let it drop (leave it, let it go) in order that your Father who is in heaven may also forgive you your [own] failings and shortcomings and let them drop. But if you do not forgive, neither will your Father in heaven forgive your failings and shortcomings."*

I like the way the Amplified version puts it. *Let it drop (leave it, let it go).* I picture myself letting go of the weight of unforgiveness I've been carrying around for all these years. Letting it drop into the hands of Jesus.

The Forgiveness Cross

An illustration that has helped me to walk through the process of forgiveness in my life is the forgiveness cross. It represents three different parts of forgiveness as you can see below.

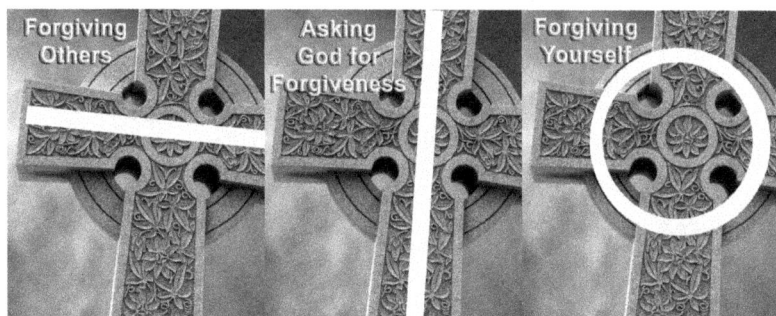

1. Forgiving Others

2. Asking God for Forgiveness

3. Forgiving Yourself

Therefore, this book is broken down into three different sections where real people share their true stories of forgiveness in their lives as it relates to forgiving others, asking God for forgiveness and forgiving yourself.

We pray that their stories offer you hope in your current circumstances. We've also provided questions for reflection after each section so that you can apply what you're reading to your own life for deeper healing and freedom in Christ.

"It is for freedom that Christ has set us free. Stand firm, then, and do not let yourselves be burdened again by a yoke of slavery."

~Galatians 5:1

Part One:
Forgiving Others

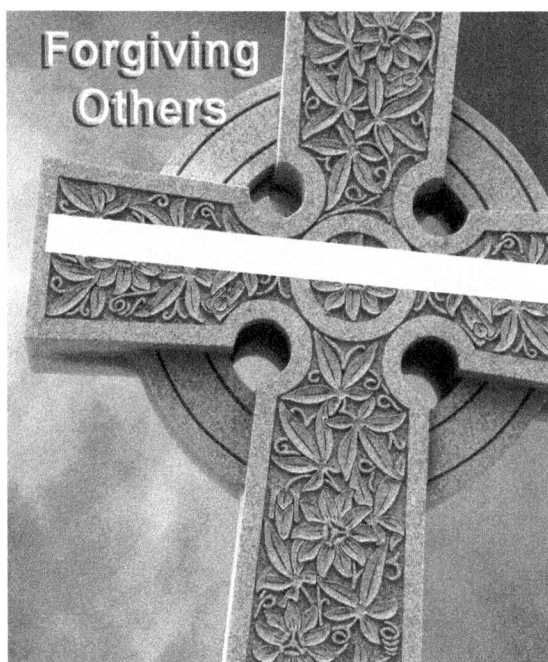

Freedom in Christ

Submitted by Gwen Ebner

It seems that forgiveness is, and has become, a necessary habit in my life.

~Forgiving my father for being emotionally unavailable to me...

~Forgiving my mother for being so controlling...

~Forgiving my grieving grandmother for shutting me out, favoring my older sister, and rejecting me now that Grandpa was gone...

~Forgiving the boyfriend who rejected and betrayed me and hurt me so deep...

~Forgiving the policeman who took my father-in-law to jail (thinking he was drunk when he had had a stroke) and left him alone all night in a cell to continue having strokes and then consequently die...

~Forgiving the man who my mother-in-law remarried who strangled her to death, thinking in his confused mind he was helping her...

~Forgiving the college girl who was driving and had an accident with a truck that took the life of my eighteen year old niece...

~Forgiving the woman in the van who struck my fourteen year old nephew on a bike, taking his life...

~Forgiving the friend who betrayed me with my husband...

~Forgiving the man who brutally beat that husband who now has to live with permanent brain damage all of his life...

On and on it goes: forgiving the person who stole my car, the person who stole my purse, the relative that cheated me out of money, the hurtful remarks from Christian friends, and the drunk that hit me sitting still at a stop sign which resulted in a lifetime of neck and shoulder pain. Forgiving... forgiving... forgiving... and probably more forgiving still to come!

But I Am Free Because I Have Been Able to Forgive

Thankfully I had a great model that showed me how and why to forgive; it was Jesus. He forgave when he was rejected, misunderstood, betrayed, brutally beaten, unjustly treated, killed, and dying in pain. And the best part is that he forgave those outrageous acts so that I could live free in this life – free from bitterness, sin, fear, and hopelessness.

What a blessing to be able to forgive! It has set me free to experience the joy of living!

"Consider it a sheer gift, friends, when tests and challenges come at you from all sides. You know that under pressure, your faith-life is forced into the open and shows its true colors. So don't try to get out of anything prematurely. Let it do its work so you become mature and well-developed, not deficient in any way."

~James 1:2-4, MSG

The Power of Forgiveness

Submitted by Renee Johnson Fisher

"If another believer sins against you, go privately and point out the offense. If the other person listens and confesses it, you have won that person back."

~Matthew 18:15, NLT

Forgiveness.

The Bible is pretty clear on forgiving others. With Matthew 18:15-18 as our guidebook, we are shown how to go directly to the person and show them if they have wronged you.

I Love How Proactive the Bible is on Forgiveness.

Maybe it's because the root of bitterness grows so easily.

I tell you–after Marc and I moved into our new house we quickly realized how challenging our front lawn would prove to be. Those devil grass roots (also known as Bermuda) are tough. They don't die for just anyone or anything. They need to be sprayed with Round Up numerous times. And you have to wait TWO WEEKS between each spray.

Not to mention we have the pressure of the HOA breathing down our neck.

But isn't that real life?

We have the pressures of this world and others treating us unfairly. We pray for mercy and grace and yet seem to come up empty. Meanwhile the soil of our hearts grows bitter as we choose unforgiveness.

This Week, Refuse to Allow Others to Rob You of the Joy Found in Jesus. Allow the Spirit to Help You Find and Give Forgiveness.

Quickly.

"If another believer sins against you, go privately and point out the offense. If the other person listens and confesses it, you have won that person back. But if you are unsuccessful, take one or two others with you and go back again, so that everything you say may be confirmed by two or three witnesses. If the person still refuses to listen, take your case to the church...I tell you the truth, whatever you forbid on earth will be forbidden in heaven, and whatever you permit on earth will be permitted in heaven."

~Matthew 18:15-18, NLT

But Wait There's More!

"I also tell you this: If two of you agree here on earth concerning anything you ask, my Father in heaven will do it for you. For where two or three gather together as my followers, I am there among them."

~Matthew 18:19-20, NLT

I Love How God Confirms and Then Expands on the Words He's Already Planted in Our Hearts for it is Strong Enough to Save Our Souls (James 1:21, NLT).

One of the strongest and most powerful lessons I've ever learned in Scripture came from that very Scripture in James.

I literally took God at his Word.

And when I did, He healed me.

I'll never forget the day I couldn't forgive myself for the lack of skin on my face and feet. I had tried everything: been to doctors, even stayed overnight in the hospital a few times, took cortisone cream... No matter what I did my eczema still refused to cooperate. I couldn't forgive myself or God for allowing me to suffer. Even though I knew I was doing good I still had to wait. My goodness didn't, couldn't, nor could ever guarantee God's healing.

Like I said earlier, God is sovereign.

It is up to Him to heal.

Or not.

So I waited.

Then one day God told me to act. Quickly. He told me to get rid of all my cortisone creams. This was the only thing saving me and my skin (and my sanity). So I got it all out from underneath my bed (cue the lurking monster music) and put it in a black trash bag and gave it to my mom and told her to dump it in some dumpster and not tell me so there was no way for me to look back!

In an instant my body bag filled with death became the life that I needed.

From that moment on God healed my skin–and got all the credit (and the glory).

Friends, Forgiveness is an Active and Alive Process. We Cannot Lie Down and Allow the Roots to Grow Underneath Us.

Literally.

We have to pull them up and throw them away and move on.

"Therefore, since we are surrounded by such a huge crowd of witnesses to the life of faith, let us strip off every weight that slows us down, especially the sin that so easily trips us up. And let us run with endurance the race God has set before us. We do this by keeping our eyes on Jesus, the champion who initiates and perfects our faith. Because of the joy awaiting him, he endured the cross, disregarding its shame. Now he is seated in the place of honor beside God's throne"
~ Hebrews 12:1-2, NLT

Well, what are you waiting for?

Get rid of it already!

There's power enough to save your soul.

Forgiving is Hard

Submitted by Staci Stallings

One of the most difficult things about being a mom is walking your children through life's really tough lessons. You can be floating along just fine, never even seeing the storm clouds gathering, when suddenly you're caught in a maelstrom. That's what happened the other day with my son. Now he's eight and very softhearted. He makes it a point to be nice to everyone (other than, of course, his two sisters). He takes things in very deeply. No surface living for him! He's also highly creative and he wants to be acknowledged for the good ideas he comes up with. Sometimes that's a challenge in second grade. (Okay, it doesn't get any easier after second grade either, but we'll deal with that later.)

So the other day he gets in the van after school. I asked how his day was and he said, "Bad." Now he has "April Fooled" me numerous times coming back with "not really, it was great!" But not this time. No, this time, bad went from bad, to really bad, to absolutely horrible in a matter of a heartbeat.

"Mom, Anna* stole my idea!" (*not her real name)

"What do you mean she stole your idea?" I asked.

"I had this idea to make a big card for one of the teachers from the whole class, and she stole my idea. She told the teacher about it, and the teacher was all happy and excited and saying what a good kid she was. It wasn't her idea! It was MINE!" By now big crocodile tears were rolling down his little cheeks.

"Well, maybe she didn't mean to steal it. Maybe she just thought it was a good idea," I countered.

"Then why didn't she say it was mine. She just let them think it was hers." He folded his arms, "I'm not going to sign that big card. It's not fair! I'm going to just make my own and see how they like that."

"Now, sweetheart, I realize you're upset..."

"And next time I'm going to steal one of her ideas and not tell anybody it was hers. Then she can see how this feels. I bet she won't like it very much," my son went on. You really can't make this stuff up, you know?

"Listen, I don't know why she did it, but think about it this way, the teacher really liked your idea even if she was the one that said it."

"Yeah, but they think it was hers, and they're all, 'Oh, that's such a great idea. You're so smart.' I bet she'd be mad too if I took her idea like that and didn't tell anybody. I'm going to do that to her and see how she likes it."

That's when I realized he was really going to need some help getting through this. It wasn't just a thing he was going to get through. He wouldn't forget it in five minutes. This was real to him. He was angry and hurt, and carrying that around wasn't going to do anyone any good. So I said, "I think you're going to have to try to forgive her."

14

"Forgive her? Mom! She doesn't deserve to be forgiven! Besides I want to get even with her. I want her to feel like I do right now."

"I know, but that's not good for you. That is just going to make you mad and miserable. It's not going to change what happened at school," I tried.

"But it's not fair, Mom. That was my idea and no one even knows that!"

"I know, and I don't know why she took your idea without telling anyone. Maybe she just thought it was a good idea and mentioned it. Maybe she didn't mean to steal it, it just happened."

"Well, I'm still mad at her."

"I know. But I think maybe you should think about trying to forgive her–even if she doesn't deserve it. You know, we've talked about forgiveness at home. When you say you're sorry or they say they're sorry."

"But she didn't even say she was sorry. I don't even think she is."

"You're probably right, maybe she isn't even sorry, but that doesn't mean you can stay mad. It's still important to forgive her... for you," I explained

"But, Mom. Forgiving is hard! I don't want to forgive her. I want to be mad at her."

"I know. Forgiving is hard. That's why a lot of the time we have to ask God to help us to forgive because if it was up to us, we'd just stay mad all the time. But that doesn't fix anything. It just makes us sad, and mad, and hurt. That's no fun. But God will help you to forgive her even though it's hard." About this time the tears stopped, and I could see peace come over him. "Just think about it," I said.

You know, forgiving is hard. And the worse whatever the other person did, the harder it is to forgive. But when it's right and you know it's right, but it's hard, that's when you know you need God. God is there to help you and guide you through those rough patches when you really don't want to do the right thing, when doing the wrong thing sure sounds easier and more logical. But God's logical way will help you find real peace. The other is just a long road of misery.

By the time we got home that night, my son was in much better spirits and the next day he not only signed the big card, he included his little card with it. So maybe he learned a good lesson. I know I did.

Forgiving an Unfaithful Spouse

Submitted by Janet Perez Eckles

He came home from work one evening and, with a cold and indifferent tone, not at all typical for him, my husband Gene frowned and cleared his throat. "Let's go for a ride, we need to talk."

His demeanor, somber and aloof puzzled me.

I threw on my bright red sweater and off-white corduroy pants. I don't know why, but details of the clothing I wear in moments of intense emotion are vividly engraved in the depths of my memory. I rushed to comb my hair and joined him as he silently walked me to the car. He opened the door, and I slipped into the passenger's seat. Clueless about what he wanted to talk about, I clicked on my seat belt. He started the engine and we rode silently as the car took us out of our neighborhood without any specific destination.

The Betrayal

"What's wrong?" I finally asked, my hand sweaty and my stomach tight.

He drew in a long breath and spat words that seared my soul, "I'm not happy …I've been wanting to tell you this for a long time." I held my breath, "There's another person in my life." His tone rang sad and at the same time indifferent, "She works with me and I've been confiding in her." The words that followed scorched my ears and stabbed rejection into my stomach.

"I don't feel well," I muttered. That cold black bucket seat suddenly felt like an electric chair, sending painful impulses of burning bolts through me. His feeble explanations and justifications eluded me. My concentration turned to visions of me and our three little boys added to the countless homes without fathers.

Trying to Survive

As weeks swept by, my house was no longer a home, but a pile of emotional rubble. My outward silence masked the turmoil that exploded inside me.

We made one more attempt. A secular counselor advised, "No sense in continuing a relationship that has been broken."

Alone and angry, I felt I was sinking deeper into the sand of sorrow. And though I'd grown up in church, I was stuck in spiritual infancy. I believed in God superficially, but deep down, I trusted in my own abilities. I'd felt satisfied with my life which, up to then, had followed a nearly perfect path. But now I desperately pounded through a dark alley, chased by shameful failure and rejection. With each step, I'd complain, and begged God for an answer. But His response of silence further intensified my anguish.

A Glimmer of Hope

Then, a dim light flickered through the fog when a friend invited me to her Christian church. And while sitting still, Bible teachings reached my heart and caused me to listen, really listen. Eventually, my sobbing stopped, and a powerful verse flung my blindfold off:

"...seek first the kingdom of God... and all these things will be added to you."

~Matthew 6:33, ESV

I had been seeking my husband's love, his devotion, and the restoration of our marriage-that had been first in my list of priorities, not God. I swallowed hard in blatant awareness of my mistake, and I vowed to obey Him, no matter what.

Looking back, I had wondered about God's silence. But now, I realize He wasn't silent at all, it was my relentless ranting that drowned out His loving whisper. It was the forceful focus on my pain that blinded me from seeing the way out.

My New Path

And now, with a clear view of my new path, my anger and self-pity turned to constant prayer for my husband. Renewed security in God fluttered through my heart. And instead of tormenting thoughts, sleep came back at night as well as calmness during the day. Diligent application of Bible verses gave me renewed clarity and focus.

Though I blinked tears back, courage and confidence nudged me to address the issue once again. But this time, rather than a confrontation, I vowed it would be a peaceful dialogue.

"I didn't force you to marry me," I said with outward calmness. "And I won't force you to stay either," my heart thumped. "Jesus will be the Father our sons might not have, and He will be the husband who'll never leave me."

An Unbelievable Turn of Events

Some days went by. Gene came home and asked to talk. He clasped my hand and held it tight, "I made a decision too." He said with conviction in his voice, "I will continue with our marriage. I'll be devoted to you and the kids."

Though my heart did a cartwheel, I held my words. Unlike before, my emotions wouldn't guide my reactions. Instead, God's wisdom would allow my response to glide with wisdom and poise. I accepted his decision, but caution still whispered way inside. I wasn't sure his words would turn to actions, but when he followed through I put another condition-that we needed to make a drastic change; we'd have to pray together.

He agreed.

The Most Difficult Hurdle

I heaved a deep sigh and braced myself to jump the most difficult hurdle-to forgive him. The choice was clear-nurse that wound, continue to look at it, dwell on it, and keep it fresh-or forgive, heal and watch it disappear. I chose the latter. And when I did, sweet freedom ushered in. The window of joy let in a fresh breeze of confidence. Gene wasn't married to that insecure young woman anymore. Forgiveness had dressed me with security, dignity and grace.

As we plan our next anniversary, celebrating 36 years of marriage, we dance to the melody of God's Word. Gene took the first step of repentance, and I followed with firm strides of forgiveness.

And to my delight, we still follow the rhythm of God's symphony directing our renewed marriage fueled with revived romance.

Mercy for a Murderer

Edited excerpt from "Angels in the Landfill"

Submitted by Carlynn

Ineradicable in my memory is the horrific moment, on Palm Sunday, when my brother found me and gently told me of my daughter's death.

Upon hearing the news of the coroner's call, I asked rhetorically:

"He killed her, didn't he?" referring to her fiancé, Antonio. Little by little he'd isolated her, as abusers do, and by the time she died she was a prisoner in her own home. I grabbed my thirty-eight revolver, an extra clip, and my Bible and said: *"let's go."* My intention was clear; I was on a manhunt.

A Lesson in Forgiveness

As a new Christian, I wasn't familiar enough with scripture to pick out individual passages alone, so I scoured my Bible and cross–referenced the concepts of murder, vengeance and killing. On that interminable plane ride out west to bring her body home for the last time, I came to know a lot about the character of God and Jesus.

Jesus taught relentless forgiveness, (i.e. '7 times 7 times 7'), turning the other cheek, and letting God settle scores. By the time the airplane set heavily down, mimicking my own heart's weight, I realized what I was, and was not, allowed to do regarding Antonio and his inequity. The New Testament places payback squarely in God's domain alone. 'Justice is mine' saith the Lord (Rom. 12:19). And that was that; I was not permitted by highest law, to extract the vengeance I so craved.

Learning to Let Go

When Antonio got away with murder—he only spent four years behind bars—I was stunned, and I vented my raw anguish in the internet support groups for those who've lost loved ones by violence. And though I'd never be a member by choice, these victim–survivors were the only ones who understood the inconsolable agony, the flashbacks, the meltdowns near birthdays, the cruel Mother's Days without our beloveds, the legal maze, the remorse, blame, doubt, and intense yearning.

The various groups for trauma survivors have made huge strides in legal advocacy and continue to fight for victims' legal rights, as well as give solace to the grieving. But after awhile with these fellow online and local survivors, I was astonished that some had spent their entire lives consumed with a burning thirst for justice and the outcome of a murderer's fate, all at incredible cost. Sustaining that level of vehemence is exhausting, life–sapping, and often futile. For them it may have been healing, a way to focus their anger and avenge their loved ones, but for me it was like a wayward seed sewn in rock or a crooked, rancorous branch unpruned. Instead, I wanted to transform from victim to victor, from bitter to better. The choice seemed clear to me: either forgive, or die spiritually. I felt God gently pushing me toward resolution, peace and life.

A Change of Heart

I began to pray for mercy for Antonio, though admittedly it was difficult initially. Honestly, I didn't really want him to feel the peace and joy that stems from knowing God; I wanted him to burn in hell – to feel and be where I'd been. Thus, it was more out of discipline that I first began these prayers, because as Christians we're told to pray for those who persecute us and those we hold dear.

So how could I dare ask God to grant me mercy and forgiveness, but withhold it from my enemy? That is not my within my realm of duty, for scripture tells us that as we judge, so are we also judged. As mercy is God's territory, I know He has it all worked out in the larger blueprint of life, which I am not privy to, and I have to contend with not knowing. I have enough faith to believe the plan exists, that His righteousness and mercy are indeed perfect and holy.

As Cicero first proclaimed: *'where there is life, there is hope.'* A beating heart is the only prerequisite for a chance meeting with God, an alternate pathway, an attempt at atonement, and change. So I leave the possibility of Antonio's reconciliation and repentance open, for we know that no one is beyond God's reach. And though he's out of prison now, if his heart is still made of stone, he's not free at all; he is in bondage to evil, and I have both great pity and prayer for anyone that far removed from The Light.

As Paul reminds us in his second letter to those in Corinth (5:10) 'For we must all appear before the judgment seat of Christ, so that each one may be recompensed for his deeds in the body, according to what he has done, whether good or bad.' Antonio will eventually answer for all the ways he's darkened this world, but I'm no longer chained to that outcome. In exchange for my prayers and pleas, God granted me peace, and He took that backpack full of the toxic gunk that I'd been hauling around. That allowed me the freedom to enjoy yesterday's memories, and today's autumnal breezes and turning of the leaves. I know now that when we humans choose to forgive, often it has more to do with our relationship with our Abba than with the forgiven.

Moving Forward

Now I rarely think about Antonio at all anymore, or our bankrupt justice system, whose travesties lie in ragged heaps around us like twisted, wrecked cars in a junkyard. Yet I still pray for his redemption, with sincerity now, and it makes me – and possibly Antonio – a better person.

Some days I feel my only child with me in spirit, reminding me: *'Don't cry for me Mom, I'm OK and I'm still in your heart. Look for me in the butterflies and in the wind!'* So I arise and smile, thanking God for the day He has made, and promising to delight in it. I see Him in the birds abounding, the creek banks flowing over rocky ledges, the laughter of a child, and the resplendent forests, and I know again, that God is magnificent and omnipresent. No one can steal that joy unless I let them, and I'm holding onto it for life.

I discovered that bleak night ten years ago that there is no such thing as earthly justice; it's a myth we created in order to survive in this violent and broken place that is for now, 'home.' I sing along with Leonard Cohen's lament that life is *a cold and it's a broken hallelujah,'* (Cohen 1984), but it's a hallelujah nonetheless.

Justice is divine; it is inherently, indisputably and *only* divine. But is that enough? The answer is an unapologetic 'yes,' for His grace is entirely sufficient for me, sufficient for us all. So once again, I bow to the eastern sunrise, and whisper a ragged but resolute 'Amen.'

Forgiving a Close Friend

Submitted by Yvonne Pat Wright

We became friends over the telephone when a mutual business acquaintance gave her business card and I called her to assist me with a problem I was having. I was so impressed with her giving manner and readiness to assist I suggested that we meet to discuss some business I could put her way.

That started a friendship which is now in its fifteenth year. For most of this time it has been a warm, girly friendship, and we have shared many of the rough paths our lives have taken during that time. But there was an ominous cloud hanging, waiting to envelope the friendship and to destroy it; to separate us, and leave us bereft of that key ingredient all humans seek...*friendship.*

I have learned that my girlfriends are not going to be paragons of virtue, we may not value the same things, our ideas may vary widely, and we will disagree on a lot of things. But somewhere in ourselves, when we find a kindred spirit that is able to share, empathies and care for us when it matters most, that is what I seek from my friends.

Rising Tension

There is much tension in the relationship between this friend (whom I will call Yolanda), and her sister. A lot of this manifests in jealousy, and after a short time in each others' company, any cordiality wanes to be replaced with antipathy. I met her sister many years into my friendship with Yolanda, and she too became my friend. My friendship with both sisters was compartmentalized and we never shared in activities together, making it easy for what ensued to occur. There were many rifts and both shared their side of the story with me. I was careful to be impartial and not take sides. At times I felt that both were vying to be especially nice to me to what end I've never found out.

Round about 2007, there was a change in Yolanda's attitude towards me, and she became very precise and not her normal friendly self. I knew she was going through a tough time in her personal affairs, so I put it down to distraction because of this. I was busy getting on with my life and beginning to write my book, so I too could have been a little casual with the friendship.

During this time her sister was becoming much more ingrained in my life and I enjoyed her. She has a lovely Christian attitude and while I was going through a miserable depressive episode; she was a very calming and soothing influence. I'm not sure when she began to drop hints about the things her sister had been saying about me. It may have been in response to me relating a hurtful incident Yolanda had enacted. Notwithstanding that, I know now that I should never have listened. The Bible warns us about having itching ears, and the things we should give heed to, but I did not object, and soon, a whole raft of things were revealed. Things I had shared with this friend whom I had taken into my confidence were being repeated to me with an unflattering spin, and reports of acrimonious statements made by her hurt me deeply.

I found it hard to believe that these things been said by someone whom I had held as my dear friend. It was painful because Yolanda was someone I had opened myself up to and been very vulnerable with. She too had confided deep things with me, which I would never have thought to reveal. To say I was hurt would be an understatement. Yet, I listened, absorbed it all and wept bitterly. Later as I poured out my heart to the Lord, He reminded me that He too had been betrayed by a close friend. I took comfort that I had been considered worthy to suffer like my Lord did.

The Dividing Rift

I had to make a decision. I knew that if I confronted her, this would cause an even greater rift between the sisters. So I made the decision that I would never repeat to her what I had been told, neither would I let on how I had been hurt and felt so betrayed. I decided that I would withdraw from her. If she wondered why, she never asked or tried to find out, adding grist to my mill that she was a false friend.

The estrangement lasted almost two years. Often I prayed and asked the Lord to help me forgive, while being careful not to harbor any resentment. I tried to put her out of my mind, but deep down I missed her and the great times we shared. The Lord would not let me forget her, and as I would get little tidbits of what was going on with her from her sister, I could not completely forget her.

Reconciliation

I was constantly being reminded that if I did not forgive, my Heavenly Father would not forgive me, and that taking my gifts to the altar was unacceptable, until I had made my peace with my friend. I remember making the decision to forgive her. I knew I could forgive her, but I knew that I also needed to reconcile with her and that was what I found difficult to follow through with. Why was reconciliation necessary? Because I believe that in a situation like this, we have not truly forgiven unless we allow ourselves to become vulnerable with the person, to the point that they can hurt us again. That is hard to put into practice.

Midway into the second year of our estrangement, her sister told me that she was ill and admitted to hospital. The moment I heard this I knew that I could no longer hold on to my resentment; the moment for forgiveness had arrived. Thoughts of how she had cared for me following my own time in hospital came flooding back, I had to go visit her and help her in whatever way I could.

Happily, she only spent two nights in the hospital and as soon as she got home, I telephoned and said I was coming round to visit. She did not feel up to visitors at the time so we arranged for a day later in the week. So it was, about four days later, armed with gifts of fruits and juice I returned to the home where I had enjoyed great times, meals, and fun. At first the conversation was strained, but gradually as we talked about the circumstances of her illness and tried to catch up on what was happening in each others' lives at the time, the atmosphere became lighter and the conversation grew warmer. Eventually the talk got round to the separation, and we agreed that we were happy to resume the friendship. I made one stipulation though, that if we were going to reconcile, and since it was accepted that I was the one who had withdrawn, I was never going to say what had caused the rift. And so it has been in the nearly two years since the friendship has been restored.

A Friendship to be Thankful For

I have had reason to be so thankful to the Lord that I had been obedient to His leading and forgiven and reconciled to my friend, to the extent of making myself vulnerable to be hurt, but that is what we are asked to do. Earlier this year (2011) she lost her husband who died suddenly. This was an extremely traumatic and stressful time for her and the children. She needed a lot of support and, in particular, she had no one else but me to call on for comfort and prayers. In God's long term plan for our lives, He knew that she would need me at that sad time, and that I would be the only person available to meet the spiritual needs, and that was why He was so insistent that I be obedient and forgive without recrimination. How would it have been if I had not been there for her to minister to her deepest needs at such a critical time?

The friendship is restored as if it had never been broken, and she has asked that we pledge never to let anything come between us again. And to that I say, *Amen*.

Relationships, Self-Harm and Forgiveness

Submitted by Sarah Deschatelets

When I was 13 years old, I got my first boyfriend. I don't know why I dated him; I didn't really like him. I think I was so desperate to have someone love me that I didn't care who the love was from. You see, my biological dad has never been in the picture; he shows up in my town every once in a while and expects me to just drop everything and pretend he's the world's greatest dad. That's never been easy for me, and when I was 13, I just wanted someone to love me.

A Relationship That Ended Badly

Back to that first boyfriend... Well, the 'relationship' lasted a few weeks and ended pretty badly. For about a month after him and I broke up, every time I would log onto Facebook or MSN I would have a message from him or some of his friends telling me how ugly I was, that I was fat, that I was stupid, they called me names that I won't mention.

This boy and his friends took every bit of self-esteem that I had, and absolutely tore it apart. I didn't tell anyone what was happening. I didn't have anyone that I thought I could trust. I kept all of the bad feelings I had developed about myself inside and didn't let anyone know that I was feeling terrible.

The Self-Hate and Self-Harm Began

The self-hate that I had just kept getting worse, even after those boys stopped sending me messages. I ended up starting to self-harm. I felt that no one could love me. I felt that I was fat. I felt that I was ugly. I felt like I deserved to hurt myself. Cutting reminded me that the pain and hate that I was feeling on the inside was valid since I could also see it on the outside. Cutting allowed me, for a slight moment, to feel okay about myself, and then I would go back to hating every single thing about myself.

All of the self-hate and self-harm kept going for about a year until I'd finally had enough of it. I really didn't know Jesus – I knew who He was, but I didn't know His love.

A Turning Point

Anyway, I was at a Bible camp and we were all sitting in the cabin doing devotions, and we were just asking questions and having the cabin counselor's answer. I was angry at my self-harming behaviors by then, and I just came out and asked if self-harm was a sin. Their answer, of course, was yes. Then that was it, no one mentioned self-harm for the rest of the night. The next day I went in and talked to my cabin counselors about it. Those two lovely ladies really taught me about God's love and mercy. I became a Christian that week.

I Still Struggle at Times

It's been about a year and a half since then. I still, every now and then, struggle with cutting. I still struggle sometimes with feeling resentment towards my biological dad and that first boyfriend. There are many times that I wake up in the morning and feel so much hate towards my biological dad for not being around for me, or towards that first boyfriend and his friends for treating me the way they treated me. There are still days that I really forget that I am a fearfully and wonderfully made child of God, and I forget that I do not deserve the hate I feel towards myself and that I do not deserve to hurt myself.

Forgiveness is a Process

I've learned that forgiveness really isn't always a onetime deal. Every time I realize that I am feeling resentment or hate towards my biological dad or first boyfriend, I have to bring it back to the Lord in prayer and lay all those sinful feelings down at His glorious feet. I have to let the Lord have control and I have to trust in Him.

Forgiveness hasn't been easy for me; there are times that I feel so much hate towards myself, and I start thinking back to all of the things that first boyfriend and his friends said to me, and I get angry with those boys all over again. I know that I just can't allow Satan to have control of me and allow myself to feel angry and resentful towards those people; God loves them just as much as he loves me and as Ephesians 4:32 says *"Be kind to each other, sympathetic, forgiving each other as God has forgiven you through Christ."* (GW).

Healing Dog
Submitted by CJ Hitz

"Hatred stirs up quarrels, but love makes up for all offenses."
~ Proverbs 10:12 NLT

Several years ago I heard a story of a sad-faced little girl who approached Billy Graham with a question she'd been dwelling on since losing her dog in an accident. Approaching the popular evangelist, the little girl boldly asked, "Mr. Graham, will I get to see my dog in heaven someday?" With a big smile Billy replied, "Young lady, if that would make you any happier then, yes, I believe you will." What a great answer to help lift the little gal's spirit. After all, don't all dogs go to heaven?

Shelley & I certainly know what it feels like to become attached to a dog. For three years, we had the privilege of being graced with a wonderful little short-haired Dachshund named Penny. Penny was the only dog either of us ever owned since neither of us grew up with pets. We stumbled upon Penny while searching for Dachshunds online. An adoption agency called Planned Pethood (no affiliation with Planned Parenthood) had an ad placed by Penny's owner who lived about 40 miles away.

We contacted the owner and set up an appointment to meet this little dog. Arthur had recently lost his wife and was unable to continue caring for Penny who they'd adopted only a year before to be a companion for his ailing wife. As she came rambling around the corner into the living room, Penny jumped up on the couch between Shelley & me and proceeded to go back and forth licking each of our faces. We were sold. "We'll take her Arthur."

Penny had such a loving personality and served as a great companion for Shelley during a season when I was traveling more. One day, Shelley needed to stop by our church and decided to take Penny along. While there, one of our friends overheard Shelley call out to Penny and came up to ask, "Did you say Penny?" "Yes, that's our dog's name", said Shelley. "No way!!" said our friend. "I think this is the same dog that belonged to my sister's family." "Really?", Shelley said curiously. This friend of ours called her sister right there and said with excitement, "You'll never guess who I'm standing next to...Penny!"

Indeed, this was an incredible coincidence. We found out that Penny's original owners (before Arthur & his wife) had her for nearly five years and Penny was a breeding dog who produced five litters of seven pups each time! Unfortunately, Penny began to dominate their other dogs with her strong motherly qualities so the husband decided to give Penny away...without telling the rest of the family. This was especially devastating to their little boy, Wes, who Penny would sleep with each night. Upon hearing his mom talk about Penny on the phone, he began to sob. Shelley could actually hear him saying he wanted Penny back which was heart-breaking.

Another Mission of Love

About a year and a half later, Shelley & I found ourselves traveling more together and in need of a dog sitter more often.

Penny simply wasn't a good travel dog and would panic even when we'd leave her in the car when going into the post office. She was happiest when she was warming up someone's lap at home. With Shelley & I being her third owners, I can't blame her for having separation anxiety.

We were coming upon one particular stretch where we had several trips back to back and needed to find someone to watch her for a month. But who? A few days are one thing, but a month? Shelley had an idea. "Why don't we ask Penny's original owners if they'd like to watch her?" I was feeling a little nervous about this idea when Shelley continued, "At the end of that time, we can ask them how it went and whether they'd like to keep Penny."

You have to understand what a painful prospect this was for both Shelley & I. We were so attached to that little dog and had planned to be her last owners. Even so, with more opportunities to travel and speak together, we had to face the reality that Penny might be better off in another home.

Penny's original owners were thrilled to watch her for us and we were excited as well. Unfortunately, Wes' father had passed away a couple years before after battling Lou Gehrig's disease so this would serve as a special reunion for young Wes and Penny. We checked in with them a couple weeks later and things were going very well. Upon seeing Penny for the first time in four years, Wes had exclaimed, "Penny's breath still smells the same!"

At the end of that stretch, we realized what we needed to do. In so many ways, Penny was a ray of sunshine that we feel

Jesus (yes, I believe he uses animals) used during an up and down three years. When we asked this family if they'd like to keep Penny, they didn't hesitate. Penny would be moving on to her next mission of love.

Licking A Wound

Several months later, we received a message from Wes' mom saying what a blessing it had been to have Penny back and how quickly she adjusted. But the most touching part of her message came when she described the healing taking place in her son's heart. For the first time, Wes had been able to express forgiveness toward his late father for giving Penny away years before. Apparently, Wes had approached his mom on his own and expressed how he no longer held a grudge toward his dad.

I know Penny's time on earth will eventually come to an end. But I'd sure like to believe she'll come running around the corner when I get to heaven someday.

One Incident that Haunted Me for Years

Submitted by RaeLynn DeAngelis

As a child I was very shy, the complete opposite of my sister who was a social butterfly. She made friends easily and had no reservations about spending the night with family and friends. I, on the other hand, experienced anxiety when it came to spending time away from home. Occasionally I spent the night with close friends, but I had no desire to spend the night at my grandparents – Their house was old and eerie. The thought of sleeping there made me very uneasy. Later I would come to understand why.

At age ten, I finally convinced myself that it was okay to spend the night with them. After all, my sister slept over several times – what could possibly go wrong? ...A decision I would later come to regret.

What Happened Next Would Change My Life Forever

My grandma taught piano lessons during the day, and my grandpa was busy doing something down in the basement; so I sat in the kitchen watching television – a game show called Hollywood Squares was playing. It's strange how some memories are sealed into your memory bank forever. A sound, a smell, or even an image can bring your mind back to that moment as if it were taking place all over again.

I could hear my grandpa's footsteps coming up the basement stairs and panic set in. For some reason I didn't like being alone with him. He made me very uncomfortable. As a child,

I felt ashamed for having these feelings because everyone seemed to love my grandpa. However, as an adult, I can now look back and see some definite warning signs leading up to this particular incident – an event that would change the course of my life forever.

There, in the kitchen, with my grandmother only two rooms away, my grandpa molested me. This was someone who was supposed to protect me, someone who I loved and trusted. I felt horrible and wanted to go home immediately. My grandpa kept apologizing and pleading for me to not tell anyone. Over and over he made me promise that I wouldn't tell.

Our Family Secret

I called my mom and asked her to come and get me. On the way home my mom could tell that something was very wrong, and so she kept prodding me to find out what was bothering me. Once we got home, I couldn't hold it back any longer.

I felt horribly guilty for betraying my grandpa by telling my mom what happened. In some strange way I felt like the villain – not the victim. I made my mom promise she wouldn't say anything because I didn't want my grandpa to know I betrayed him. How ironic. I think my mom understood how desperate and confused I felt and finally agreed not to say anything. She, instead, assured me that I would never be alone with him again.

I Wondered if my Mom Believed Me

After all, my grandpa was her father. Then years later, my mom told me about a similar incident that took place with my younger cousin. I finally received validation that my mom believed me; but along with it came a new sense of guilt – guilt wondering if I could have somehow prevented my cousin's incident. Did my secrecy jeopardize the safety of her and perhaps others?

For Years This Incident Haunted Me

I had deeply rooted hate towards my grandpa. He stole my innocence. I hated him, and I hated myself for having these feelings towards him. No one ever confronted my grandpa about this incident; he went to his grave believing I had kept the secret.

And so, negative feelings bottled up inside me for many years. The mere thought of the incident caused me great anxiety. My heart raced and fear set in every time the memory played out in my mind.

Living in Bondage to Bulimia

This tragic experience influenced some poor decisions made throughout my life. For twenty-five years I lived in bondage to an eating disorder called bulimia. I truly believe that my extremely low self-esteem following this incident was a contributing factor to me choosing that path of self-destruction. Negative feelings manifested into self-abuse and hatred.

Now the Good News...

Eight years ago, God set me free from bulimia and helped me forgive both myself and my grandpa. I didn't receive traditional help for overcoming these debilitating strongholds, but rather I was ministered to by the Great Physician and Wonderful Counselor – Jesus Christ. Through His indescribable love, forgiveness, compassion, mercy, and the truth of His Word, my chains were broken and I found true forgiveness and lasting healing.

Years later God brought me to the following Scripture.

"But if anyone causes one of these little ones who believe in me to sin, it would be better for him to have a large millstone hung around his neck and to be drowned in the depths of the sea."

~Matthew 18:6

As I read these words, a wave of compassion swept over me towards my grandpa. At that moment I realized true forgiveness had taken place. Forgiveness is a choice. When we do not forgive, we hurt ourselves more than anyone else.

Unforgiveness is like cancer; it spreads into other areas of our lives and eats away little by little. But true forgiveness is possible, and restoration will follow as long as we cling to our Lord and Savior, Jesus Christ.

"Jesus looked at them and said, "With man this is impossible, but with God all things are possible."

~Matthew 19:26

Survivor of Sexual Abuse

Submitted by Chris Tian

I see you. You are so young, so innocent, so trusting. You look up to me with eyes so full of trust. It makes you happy that I serve God, speak of love and shower you with affection. I hold your hand and begin to invite you to spend the afternoon with just me. Your own father is absent from your life, and when you call me Father it almost rings true.

Soon, I'm not just holding your hand, I am hugging you and placing my hands around you. I tell you that a little kiss would be okay and my hands move down someplace else. I take you for long walks and to the beach...always a secluded beach. "It's okay," I tell you, "just call me Father."

I sometimes cry, I sometimes sob, yet I can't stop touching you, I can't stop from kneeling down before you while I tell you, "It's okay, just call me Father."

You try to keep away from me, but your mom doesn't know our secret, and I told you not to tell her because it would hurt her real bad. Besides, "it's okay," I say, "just call me Father."

They seem to know, they somehow find out, and without ever saying good-bye, I am transferred to another parish, one I know I will like more because it is at a Catholic junior/high school. "It's okay," I tell myself, "they'll all call me Father."

***

I saw you. You were supposed to be someone I could believe in, and learn about God from. I looked up to you with eyes so

43

full of trust. It made you happy that I was blind to your ways, to your sickness and depravity, because you always pointed out that you served God, and spoke of love, and showered me with the physical affection that I yearn for from a father. You'd hold my hand and begin to lie, and manipulate me, as I would spend the afternoon with just you. You knew that my own father was absent, and when I would call you Father I had really wished it rang true.

Soon, you were not just holding my hand, you were hugging me and placing your groping hands all over me. You'd tell me that a little kiss is okay, though I never wanted you to. You assaulted me on long walks and at the beach...always a secluded beach. "It's okay," you'd tell me, "just call me Father."

I'd cry, I'd sob, yet you wouldn't stop touching me and I couldn't stop you from kneeling down before me while you told me, "It's okay, just call me Father."

I tried to keep away from you, but my mom didn't know of your sick, filthy secret, and you threatened me if I told her, or anyone, because you would hurt her real bad. Besides, "it's okay," you'd say, "just call me Father."

They seemed to know, they somehow found out, and without ever saying sorry, you were transferred to another parish, one you knew you really wanted to continue your addiction, because it was at a Catholic junior/high school. "It's okay," I told myself, "I no longer will call him Father."

***

The alcohol, drugs, self-harm incidents, my trust issues and other relational injuries nearly cost me my life. I found life anew through Christ Jesus and by walking through some long and painful inner healing.

I can never forget, yet I can forgive and while yes, I would give him a second chance, yet I wouldn't let him be tempted or tested by giving him complete access to another little boy.

Mikayla's Story
Submitted by Antonia Faisant

My husband and I were married for about 4 years when I felt a nudge to have children. I became pregnant in February of 2005, and I gave birth to Mikayla in November of that year. I had a perfectly normal pregnancy. I went to all my doctor appointments and never had any issues. I took Lamaze classes with my husband and we were so happy and looked forward to her birth. I decided that I would like to try and have Mikayla naturally in hopes all would be well.

My husband and I were very active in ministry at the time. We had planted a church in my hometown and all was well. I had people praying over the both of us (my daughter and I), and my family and friends were actively praying too.

5 days past the due date, my water broke early in the morning. I knew I had to call the hospital and be admitted because it is standard protocol to get to the hospital as soon as possible after your water breaks to avoid infection.

A lot of Things Were Going Wrong

As soon as I got to the hospital it seemed as though a lot of things were going wrong. First, the epidural was painful and I was told that if done properly that it would not be like that. Well, it ended up that the epidural had to be taken out and reinserted because the line got blocked by blood. I kept complaining about pain and they kept giving me more pain medicine and finally someone noticed the line was blocked. So I actually felt the labor for about 11 hours. I was in labor for 24 hours when it was time to have Mikayla because I was finally fully dilated.

I tried having Mikayla for about a half hour when I was told that she was under distress and it was time to remove her by c-section. I was okay with it as I wanted what was best for my little girl. They prepped me for surgery right away. At the time I was so tired, but I still remembered, although foggily. My husband was there the whole time and I bounced off of him concerning anything I didn't understand or know. I was awake the whole time I was in surgery, but shook terribly and even got sick. I remember the medical staff taking her out and glancing over at her as my husband let me know she was in my line of sight. He was taping the event when the doctors told him to stop.

Something Wasn't Right

Everything was happening so fast, but I found out later that she was not breathing. They had to perform CPR on her to bring her back. It was 8 minutes before we heard any baby cries. My mom was very upset as she waited outside as she saw and heard all kinds of commotion. She knew something was wrong. I just wanted to stop shaking, but it did not cease for another hour after the surgery when I waited in a recovery room. The doctor came in to talk to my husband and I and let us know that something had happened, but we would not know the extent until later.

After I got settled into my room I was able to go and see Mikayla. I remember using a wheelchair to get to her and have alone time with her. I held her hand and just looked at her. She was the only baby hooked up to medical devices. Shortly afterward I was told she was having seizures and would stop breathing each time this happened. This occurred about 4 times and the hospital staff decided she needed more care. She was going to be taken by ambulance to a hospital 45 minutes away. They brought her in my room about 10 pm that night and I remember the atmosphere. They brought her in an incubator and took her out of it so I could hold her.

I Was in Shock

I've told this story many times, and will never forget how I was in shock and thought why did this happen to me, but despite being in shock I felt the presence of God. It was like being in that middle state of action and rest. It's hard to explain, but for anyone who has ever felt this I am sure you will know exactly what I am talking about. I remember some family members were in the room with me when this happened and they were very sad. I just sat there. I gave Mikayla back to the nurses and entrusted my little girl into the hands of God.

I found out later that she seized and stopped breathing again on the way to the hospital and on the highway and also as they drove into the parking lot of the hospital.

My husband drove to the hospital alone that night and was there for Mikayla right away. I had to stay back because I needed to recover from the surgery. I eagerly waited and anticipated being able to hold her once again. Mikayla was born on Wednesday and I wasn't released from the hospital until Saturday morning. I remember having a slow recovery.

My husband had to help me (as well as) Mikayla as we both dealt with separate issues. I remember John wheeling me through the hospital for a few days and helped me wherever I was at. I stayed with some friends from Toledo for one night and the rest of the time John and I stayed at the Ronald McDonald House. Mikayla was in the NICU for 12 days. She was diagnosed with Cerebral Palsy and Epilepsy.

My Initial Response Was, "Why?"

As I look back, I have to tell you my initial response was shock and to think, 'why?' I personally think it's a natural response to a very tragic and very surprising event. I wrestled with many thoughts and have revisited this event many times since, but one thing I know is God has kept me level headed despite the odds. He has also helped me heal and not play the blame game.

One thing I have to note about my personality is that I am a realist: I see what is in front of me and deal with it accordingly. I have a clear understanding that we live in a broken world with broken people. I am certain that what happened was not intentional, it happened and now I have to deal with what I have been handed and that is it.

I Could Have Become Bitter

Many times I've had people tell me why don't you sue the hospital? I am thinking why? I am not a bitter person. I don't feel that someone owes me anything. How could I attack a hospital or a doctors' name and reputation because I can't deal with this? It would not be fair, and I would not do that to someone. Seriously two wrongs do not make things right. I will not play God by trying to figure out someone's intent. It happened this way and I believe the medical staff did what they could. Life happened.

Just this year it has finally dawned on my husband and I that Mikayla will not catch up developmentally for a long time, if ever. I deal with what is really happening, but my faith still hopes that God would help her. Should He heal her, I would love that and will hope for it. Should it not happen, I am okay with that too. God in His goodness will be right there with me through it all. God promises His faithful hand, but doesn't promise we will not go through difficult things (things we might not understand at the time). Our fallen world is evident, but His love helps us through it all.

I have so many (too many) life testimonies of His love, faithfulness, mercy, goodness, kindness, hope, joy, prayers heard, dreams fulfilled, promises fulfilled, and emotional healings. I bank on them. They have been tried and proven and handled in and through Him.

My Trust is in Christ

I trust Him daily. Some days I get a glimpse of how close He really is. Just last night I had a dream that was telling me to do something and it dawned on me, as I did what the dream was telling me, that it was a clear reminder of His grace and closeness to me in my life.

God calls us to let go and give all things to Him; His grace is sufficient. He provides way more than all that baggage could. He ultimately brings "hope" to every situation. No matter how bad things get, you can be certain of one thing, you cannot lose with God.

God Works Things Out for Our Good

I love how He works out things for our good. As a result of this, I had in my heart to start a parent support group for parents with special needs children. At first I was thinking I was going to have it be specific to my daughter's condition(s), but changed my mind seeing that many diagnoses often overlap. I was waiting on the right opportunity, and when I saw something in someone and approached her about facilitating it, it was a go.

To be honest I could have provided some kind of support, but the person I chose had so much more to offer. I just knew I had to be a constant to launch and keep this thing going. I am happy to note it has been 3 years since we first started meeting, and it is my hope that it has been a wonderful and helpful support group for all the parents that have participated. I know for me personally, it has helped me get educated, become a better advocate for my child, and I have met some wonderful friends too.

God takes the bad and makes it good, and will often use it as a wonderful help for others. Sure, some days I think, "what if?" because I am human. But there is also, "I have learned so much" and, "I have met so many wonderful people" as a result. I am choosing to look at the good, and cling to a God that I know who has always proven to be faithful.

Despite the harshness of what life can sometimes hand us we have Him and more so in the next life to come. What is 70 years of life (about the avg. life span of a man) compared to all eternity?

One day, I will see my little girl whole. Now that is an amazing thing.

Forgiving Mom

Submitted by Elaine Marie Cooper

There it was. One more criticism.

Hanging up the phone, I swallowed in defeat and resignation. Mom could never say anything without an edge of hurtful commentary. Why couldn't she ever be uplifting or supportive? All I wanted to do was share my joy and relief that I was able to successfully give an injection to a patient. Instead she replied, "Well, I learned to do that years ago for your diabetic sister." Her tone was demeaning. It hinted at, 'So what? That's not so great.'

I wanted to scream that, 'okay, it may not be so great, except that I'm terrified I won't be able to do all the skills I need to learn in nursing school.' I had a hindrance that most were not even aware I had – nerve damage in my left hand that challenged my ability to perform some procedures.

I Wasn't Born With This Disability

An accident as a child led to a progressive loss of feeling and use in my left hand. It went on for three years, accompanied by nights of intense pain. Mom had taken me one time to see our family doctor but it was not diagnosed properly. Then it was ignored.

But a trip to a surgeon's office for another concern led to an accurate assessment by an alert physician. By this time, however, the damage was permanent. While I could do some things with that hand, many movements were hindered. The worst part for me was the thin, deformed appearance of my hand. It was embarrassing then, and still is. I often hide it in various ways.

Scars from My Mom's Criticism

So Mom's words were not just hurtful, they reopened raw scars that years of her criticism had created. And her lack of response to my physical pain so many years ago had led to a lifetime of frustration and self-consciousness as I dealt with my partially crippled hand. I felt more emotionally distant from her than ever.

Never Good Enough

As far back as I could remember, I never felt like I was good enough. Mom didn't appreciate my small, childish gift of a bouquet of dandelions. When I presented them to her, she declared that they were "just weeds."

I was never thin enough. Never accomplished enough. Had children too soon after getting married. Took my kids to church too much (even though they liked it).

She always had praise for her grandchildren (thank the Lord), but somehow her own child never quite measured up. If ever I said or did something she disapproved of, she'd shake her head and say, "You're so much like me." It was not a pleasant comparison in her mind.

But Therein Lay the Problem: She Was Unhappy With Herself

That knowledge was not a comfort to me, however, when my only daughter was diagnosed with a brain tumor at the age of

23. Mom was living in California at the time and a few months later she moved to the Midwest to be nearby. It was wonderful for my daughter, as they had always been close. But it was devastating for me. At a time when I desperately needed support and encouragement, Mom was not there for me.

She'd complain to my sister that I did too much for my daughter, like help her finish a meal when the tumor hindered her ability to get the spoon easily to her mouth. Or keep her upright in her chair when she was leaning and ready to lose her balance. The problem was not that my husband and I did too much; it was that Mom could not accept my daughter's deterioration.

Within two years, my daughter passed away. Along with the aching hole in my heart, was a cavernous gap separating Mom and me.

My Ongoing Pain and Struggle

As a Christian, I knew that I needed to honor my mother. But our every interaction just seemed to increase my pain. I didn't know how to deal with it – I didn't want to deal with it, but I knew that was not an option. Mom was getting increasingly needy as her body aged and I was forced to remain involved with her. My sisters and I found a care facility to help her so that she would not injure herself or forget her much needed medications.

But my attitude kept my heart at arms' length. I knew this was not pleasing to God, so I prayed. I knew the situation might never change, but I had to be obedient to the Lord to forgive. In Ephesians 4:32 it says, *"Be kind and compassionate to one another, forgiving each other, just as in Christ God forgave you."*

My Step of Obedience and a Turning Point

Unforgiveness as a Christian is not an option, despite our feelings. Forgiving her was an act of my will, even if my heart did not feel it. I had to confess to the Lord my anger toward my mom and slowly my heart began to soften from its shield of hurt.

Then one day, an incredible conversation occurred while I was visiting her. She unexpectedly looked at me and said, "I must have been very critical of you your whole life, because when I say things to you, you get very defensive."

I tried to brush it off, but she held my eye, "No, I want you to know that I didn't mean to be so critical. And I'm sorry."

I don't even remember how I responded. I just know that I forgave her.

Mom had suffered from depression since she was small. I also knew that her own mother had not wanted her, feeling trapped with the care of a second child after her husband was killed in an accident at work. Mom never felt accepted by her own mother. That was made clear when, on the day of my mom's graduation from high school and she was valedictorian, her mother looked at her and said, "And to think I wondered what I ever did to deserve you."

I can't imagine hearing those hurtful words.

Understanding Began to Bloom

Mom began to reminisce and I listened, gleaning much-treasured information about her life and our family.

I began to write a book, a fictional account loosely based on Mom's ancestors. She was delighted. When she read it she was in awe, saying what a talented writer I was. After so many years of criticism, it felt awkward accepting praise. But I learned to accept it from her, while she learned to give it.

Our Healing Journey

So did the criticizing stop completely? No. She can still fling a few verbal arrows now and then. But those flaming words are less, and we have grown closer in these last years of her life.

If you had asked me five years ago if our relationship would ever heal, I would have said a resounding, "No." But a funny thing happened when I prayed and really gave this problem over to God – I changed, and then, so did Mom.

When Faith and Forgiveness Collide

Submitted by Julie Caulder

There is a lot that I can say about faith and there is a lot that can be said about forgiveness. Apart, both are separate and are fine on their own because they do different things in our lives.

Together, when faith and forgiveness collide, it's beautiful.

Seven months ago I began my journey with faith. I spent days and hours reading the Bible, listening to sermon after sermon and reading blog after blog, book after book trying to understand what it meant to have faith. I learned what it meant to deny ourselves and live purposely by the Spirit. However, even when I was growing in my knowledge and growing in faith, something still felt "off." It was as if one part of me was so on fire for God's Word and trying to understand what faith looked like and what it really meant, but there was still something missing.

As we grow in our faith, we begin to realize that there are things from our past that prevent us from moving forward and truly living by the Spirit. For me, there was no big moment or thing that happened, but it became apparent to me what was missing when I was contacted by someone from my past.

Then It Hit Me

Even though I had faith, I was struggling internally with forgiveness. It is only until we truly learn the power of forgiveness and what that word means in its entirety, that we can be set free and step into faith.

Some of us swear that our faith is enough and that it's sufficient. However, faith is not sufficient and cannot truly sustain us when we are unable to let go of ourselves and learn to forgive.

Forgiveness means different things to us and it's easier to say, a lot harder to do. We're human and we hold grudges. We become bitter and tainted by the lies we tell ourselves to make ourselves feel better. To make up for it, we hold on to our faith instead to sustain us and think that if we hold on tight enough, that we will somehow forget and that is what it means to forgive. Forgiveness is more than forgetting. It's more than "water under the bridge."

Forgiveness is Faith Amplified

When the person from my past contacted me I learned what it meant to forgive. The emotional and mental abuse by this person no longer mattered. This person's hateful and rude remarks about me to people in my life close to me, didn't matter. What mattered in that moment was knowing that God was working. He was working in my life. Allowing me to face my past and let go. The amazing thing about it is, I realized I already had. As I had grew in my faith and was confronted with my past in that single moment, I realized that I had inevitably "let go."

That is When Faith and Forgiveness Collided

Apart, faith and forgiveness are fine on their own and they mean different things to each person. Depending on where we are in our faith resonates a lot with how we learn to forgive and what forgiveness means with our faith strong.

Both are powerful words with different meaning. Together, faith and forgiveness are complete and so are we.

Forgiveness is a Huge Part of Love

Submitted by Heather Hart

Forgiveness is a huge part of love. I have forgiven a lot during my life, and my guess is that you have too. We can all think of some of the big things that we have forgiven, but there are countless small things that we forgive without even a second glance. One story of forgiveness that I remember occurred a couple years back when God showed me a big thing that I hadn't forgiven yet.

A Little of my Background

Before I start the story, you need to know that I am divorced; my first husband left me for another woman. While he caused me tons of heartache and made my life miserable for several years while I tried to save our broken marriage, I have completely and totally forgiven him for that. In fact, I would say that I don't even hold a grudge. That pain is in the past, and if he hadn't put me through all of that, I wouldn't be where I am today. I am practically thankful that it all happened. So where was my unforgiveness you might ask?

How My Struggle with Forgiveness Started

My unforgiveness showed up when I was talking to my son one summer day. You see, when I was pregnant with this little treasure, my ex-husband (his father), didn't want me to be. I got pregnant after he had told me that he had broken it off with the other girl that he had been cheating on me with and wanted to repair our marriage. Then, when I told him I was pregnant, instead of rejoicing, he asked me what his girlfriend was going to say. He had been lying to me, and now we were bringing a second child into the world where mommy and daddy weren't happily married. I was crushed.

However, it didn't end there. While that was the last time that I trusted him, he called me almost daily to see if I had had a miscarriage yet. 2 weeks before I was scheduled to deliver I finally lost it and told him that if I had a miscarriage at that point, it would be the last thing that he would want to ask me about. He then had the nerve to show up at the hospital for the birth of our son, and of course my mom stepped aside and let him go to delivery with me. That was the only time he has ever shown any love for our child. After that, he just kind of faded into the background. In the past 4 years, the only time he has even seen him was when the boys were visiting their grandparents (his parents) and he just happened to show up. They visit his parents only once a year, so in the last half of my little boys life, he has seen his 'father' no more than 3 times.

So on that particular summer day, my little boy was talking about his dad, and how much he loved him and missed seeing him. It was then that I realized that while I had forgiven my ex-husband for all the pain that he had caused me, I had not forgiven him for what he had done to his child. I did not believe that he deserved to be loved by such a special little boy; a little boy that he didn't even want to have in the first place.

What God Showed Me

It was during that time that God showed me that none of us deserve to be loved. Not my ex-husband, not me, not even my precious little boy. And I have to admit that I'm very thankful that God doesn't only love those that deserve His love. God loves like my child – unconditionally. His love forgives, even when we don't deserve it. We have all treated God just as my ex-husband treated my son. We have wished He wasn't there – tried to ignore His existence, we have hated Him, but He loves us anyway. I'm so thankful that He can forgive us for being so selfish, and I pray that He can help me love more like my little boy in the future.

While it wasn't easy, God used the love that my child has for the father he barely knows to help me learn to forgive my ex for the pain that he caused him. That doesn't mean that it's easy to watch my son love someone that doesn't love him back, but instead of being angry about it now, I am able to pray that God can use that same love that taught me to forgive, to reach other people for the glory of God.

One of the Hardest Things I Have Ever Done

Forgiving my ex-husband for the pain he caused (and continues to cause) my little boy was one of the hardest things that I have ever had to do. I don't know where you are, or if there is anyone that you need to forgive, but if there is, I really encourage you to do so. I hope that God can use the love of my little boy to help you understand His unfailing love that always forgives.

"Love is patient, love is kind… it is not easily angered, it keeps no record of wrongs."

~ 1 Corinthians 13:4-5

Being Sexually Abused

Submitted by Rachael Funmilayo

Forgiveness has been a theme that has often come up in my life's history and I'd like to share part of it. I happened to be brought up in an underdeveloped, rural area and grew up in a new area where there were few and scattered houses, bushes and buildings under construction and those that have been abandoned by their owners.

There was a day that I was going from my house to a neighboring house, which was some distance away, and I had to pass through bushes before getting there. A man who claimed to be one of the construction workers beckoned me to assist him in lifting some loads in an uncompleted building (you'll probably wonder what kind of load a 4-5 year old girl can lift). I followed him to the building and he violated me.

Years after, I started having some symptoms like scratching my pubic area, having copious discharges, odor, and all sorts of things. I could not speak to anyone about it all through my high school days, not until I got to college and went for a medical checkup. I was asked if I was sexually active and I told the doctor that I was a virgin. She examined me and told me I was lying because of the physical evidence. At first I did not understand, but later I remembered faintly what happened to me when I was younger.

Before then I wasn't sure whether it really happened to me or if it was just a dream. I went for series of tests and it came to a point that I was devastated because I was a young lady who people saw as a 'spiritual' sister. Having to go about the hospital doing all sorts of tests for sexually transmitted diseases and having to begin to tell the story that I was sexually abused years back was too hard for me.

Each time I had to go for tests I would cry, and cry, and my flesh would want to curse the man that violated me. It became very apparent to me at another time that I just had to let go; that whoever the man was, he needed my forgiveness. I thought of where the man would be, and what he would be doing at those times I was in pain.

In my affliction, the Word of God came to me one day that He bore all my pains, and that many are the afflictions of the righteous but God delivers him out of them all.

Forgiving this man seemed very hard to me. At times it seems like I have forgiven him, but it will just occur to me again. I walked up to a Christian friend and recalled all that I was going through as he talked to me and prayed for me for perfect healing and forgiveness. I forgave him, and today I'm perfectly healed emotionally, spiritually and physically.

Forgiveness as a Way of Life

Submitted by Dr. Chuck Sandstrom
(with Auburn Sandstrom, co-author)

In June 2009, I was executive director of a Community Foundation and a Civic Leader. While I was having an unregistered car towed from a rental property I own in Akron Ohio, I encountered the owner of the car, Michael Ayers. He was drunk and angry. He punched me in the face. My head hit a brick wall a few inches behind me at the speed of a high speed car wreck. My nose was broken, my two front teeth were knocked out, I almost died and I was unconscious for around 6 weeks. I have what is called a severe Traumatic Brain Injury or a TBI.

We lost what many would call "everything": job, new home, property, and social standing. My free-spirited wife became a 24 hour a day caregiver. Though I do continue to make progress, some of the damage will be permanent.

The surprising thing about the assault that ended our lives... is that we LIVED through it!

In January, The Akron Beacon Journal ran a front-page article in the Sunday paper about my willingness to forgive my assailant and to reach out to his family. People believe we are somehow special or saintly people to have forgiven this man.

What I want to share with you is that my wife and I are NOT abnormally good people. Trust me. But we know that the path of forgiveness can take ordinary people on an extraordinary trip.

Four things: Forgiveness is practical. Forgiveness is liberating. Forgiveness is an attitude that can be learned. Forgiveness can be a way of life.

Recovery has been a slow and difficult journey. Our hearts were broken wide open with our need for God and one another. We became outsiders to the mainstream life we had known.

We were able to see that the assailant and his family were suffering also. They too had had their lives changed overnight. Michael Ayers had gone into hiding the night of the assault and was nearly drinking himself to death. He was hiding from U.S. Marshalls who were prepared to shoot him upon arrest. He was also taking huge risks to see his children. We found out he loves and provides for his kids and they love and depend on him.

Family members were being shunned at school and work because of what Michael had done and all the press coverage about it. His son, seven-year old Michael Junior was acting up in school and flunking the third grade. Four- year old daughter Lyric was diagnosed with a serious illness. Both children cried for their father night after night.

To borrow from Harold Kushner, forgiveness is first and foremost, a way of seeing. It cannot change the facts about the world we live in, but it can change the way we *see* those *facts*.

Most people see my *injury* as a tragedy. For my wife and me, it has created an opportunity to love more deeply. Auburn says one of greatest moments of her life was a morning in November of 2009 when her husband -- just like husbands all over the world -- sat up at the edge of the bed, yawned, scratched, and headed off to the bathroom in his underwear. No nurses, no wheelchair, no breathing apparatus, no monitors, no feeding tubes. We don't take the simple miracle of being alive or of having each other to love for granted. It is an attitude we sustain each day.

When Michael was finally arrested, we realized that seeing him get sentenced, though necessary, would not bring healing. What had helped us the most had been reaching out to his family. It was like we were the first ones standing up after an earthquake and -- because our own hearts were shattered -- we wanted to help these other hurting people to stand up too. It helped us recover from our own pain.

Who among us has not been harmed by the actions of another? Who has not experienced an injustice? Who among us has not experienced -- first or second hand – a seemingly senseless tragedy. We can make tragedy make sense when we allow it to help us find our way back to each other and to a place of love.

When Michael learned that I had forgiven him, it was unbelievable to him. He told his significant other Erika he had never had such a strange feeling. He said he felt love like he'd never felt it before.

There was a moment in the court room pretrial when he turned and looked in my direction. Our eyes locked. *All either of us saw in the other's eyes at that moment was compassion.*

One Sunday, Erika arrived at our church with Michael's youngest, Baby Langston. She stood at the lectern and read a heartfelt letter of apology from Michael Ayers directly to me in front of our congregation on a Sunday when I was preaching. Some would say he was "playing us" to get a lighter sentence. We chose to be *moved* by it and, of course, to love Baby Langston!

Last spring we got involved helping little Michael Junior, the son who had been flunking the third grade. He knows me as "Dr. Chuck." The first time we picked him up he said, "You're the man who is helping my dad, aren't you. Can you please tell me why my dad is in prison?" He had heard it was for spitting on someone. It was really bugging him.

We made sure Michael Sr. had a talk with little Michael. Now he knows his dad is in prison for hurting someone but he doesn't know the person is me.

I'm happy to report that Michael Junior has made a turn-around since last spring and his teachers are pleased with his progress. We'd like to help him do more than just pass. We'd like to help him excel.

We receive weekly letters from Michael Senior. He has found faith in prison as well as help for his alcoholism. He thanks us constantly for our work with his son and tells us of his own progress.

We would like to see him get back to being a good, providing father to his kids and possibly a friend to us.

According to statistics, men like Michael Ayers don't change. His future should look like his past: Alcoholic rage, bullying and prison. It is between Michael and his own soul what path he ultimately takes in life. Our business is what is in our *own* hearts.

It was over two years ago that I incurred this brain injury and I'm not done healing yet! I'm driving, swimming and golfing. In July of 2011, I ran my first 5k.

When I was a successful pastor with 1000 plus parishioners, a thriving consulting business, a dozen investment properties and several afternoons a week to devote to golfing, I used to say, "I love my life. I'm doing what I was born to do." This sometimes struck people as presumptuous. It was like I was bragging and saying "I have it made."

Well, it true now. I have it made!

I walk funny and talk funny and have a thousand impairments, some visible, some invisible, but I am still exactly who I was made to be, doing exactly what I was born to do, saying exactly what I was born to say. And now that I have the advantage of this brain injury to say it with, people no longer think I'm just bragging!

One of our greatest joys is when this life of ours (which includes my brain injury) can serve to inspire others.

We probably wouldn't have arrived at such a surprising way of life without a knock to my head but we're glad to be in a place where we can highly recommend it to you. Not the knock in the head, but the surprising way of life!

The Way of Forgiveness: Living Forgiving

Submitted by Shelley Hitz

The story you just read about Chuck Sandstrom is the story of my dad. And on October 10, 2009, he chose to forgive Michael, the man who assaulted him. My dad's life has been changed forever through this one moment in time, and he continues to heal a little more each day from his traumatic brain injury.

On October 23, 2009, I was also faced with my own issues of unforgiveness with Michael. There were still emotions I needed to deal with: unforgiveness, bitterness, and resentment.

Here is an excerpt from my journal:

The Journey of Forgiveness God Led Me on That Day.

Lord, what about Michael?

"Let him go. Let him be judged by my courts. Let him face his true punishment. Mine. You will accomplish nothing by ensuring that he is judged severely here on earth. Pray for him. I will not let this go unjudged or unpunished. Either he will take full punishment for his crime against your dad and your family or Jesus will take it for him, just as he will take the punishment for your sins. Let Michael go. It is not your responsibility to judge him or fix him. Leave him in my hands."

"Do not judge, and you will not be judged. Do not condemn, and you will not be condemned. Forgive, and you will be forgiven. Give, and it will be given to you. A good measure, pressed down, shaken together and running over, will be poured into your lap. For with the measure you use, it will be measured to you."

~Luke 6:37-38

Romans 2:1 says, *"You, therefore, have no excuse, you who pass judgment on someone else, for at whatever point you judge the other, you are condemning yourself, because you who pass judgment do the same things."*

I know I am guilty of judging Michael.

"Shelley, I don't want you to sit in the judgment seat of Michael, let Me. I will take care of this. I want your heart to be filled with My love. Not anger, bitterness or resentment. Allow my Spirit, my light to drive out the darkness in your heart. I have called you out of the darkness and into my marvelous light. (I Peter 2:9) Let me take care of it. Trust me. Release your control of it.

For as Matthew 18:21-35 clearly says - unforgiveness places you in a prison where you will be tortured. I have set you free, forgiven you and rescued you from darkness. Don't allow this to imprison you again. Let it go. Let it go. Leave Michael to me. And trust me with what happens. Keep your eyes and your focus on Me and on your own sin. Don't get so focused on everyone else's sin. You have enough to handle of your own. It is not your responsibility to make sure justice is served. It is Mine. And whoever welcomes one of my children, welcomes

Me. Whoever messes with one of my children, messes with Me."

"Things that cause people to sin are bound to come, but woe to that person through whom they come. It would be better for him to be thrown into the sea with a millstone tied around his neck than for him to cause one of these little ones to sin. So watch yourselves."

~Luke 17:1-2

I do not take this lightly, Shelley. I will take care of Michael. Leave him to Me.

"If your brother sins, rebuke him, and if he repents, forgive him. If he sins against you seven times in a day, and seven times comes back to you and says, 'I repent,' forgive him."

~Luke 17:3-4

Shelley, my way is a way of forgiveness. It is one of the central themes of My life and ministry. As I said on the cross, *"Father, forgive them for they know not what they are doing."* (Luke 23:34) I ask you to forgive Michael, for he knows not what he has done and the depth of the pain he has caused you and your family.

"And whenever you stand praying, if you have anything against anyone, forgive him and let it drop (leave it, let it go), in order that your Father Who is in heaven may also forgive you your [own] failings and shortcomings and let them drop."

~Mark 11:25, AMP

Lord, today I choose to forgive Michael. I let go of my anger, bitterness and resentment of him - for what he has done to my dad and our family. I leave it in your hands and let it drop from mine. I trust that you will take care of this and I allow you to be the ultimate judge no matter what the earthly courts decide. I will never agree that what Michael did was right but I release him and his crime to you today. I choose the way of forgiveness and ask you to empower me to live forgiving in my actions and words towards Michael. Empower me to love my enemies and pray for those who persecute me (Matthew 5:44). Empower me to overcome evil with good (Romans 12:21).

"Do not take revenge, my friends, but leave room for God's wrath, for it is written: 'It is mine to avenge; I will repay,' says the Lord. On the contrary: 'If your enemy is hungry, feed him; if he is thirsty, give him something to drink. In doing this, you will heap burning coals on his head."

~Romans 12:19-20

Empower me Lord to live the life You have called me to live. I pray that you would take care of Michael...his judgment, his crime and his soul. I pray you would be working in his life and his heart to bring him to You. This would truly be a miracle, Lord.

"Do not repay evil with evil or insult with insult, but with blessing, because to this you were called so that you may inherit a blessing."

~1 Peter 3:9

Thank you Lord for what you are doing in my heart, setting me free from this unforgiveness, bitterness and resentment.

Thank you for empowering me through Your Holy Spirit to walk this out every day, even when I don't feel like it.

I praise You Lord for all the miracles we are seeing in Dad's life and the physical, emotional and spiritual healing you are bringing to him.

"You (Michael) *intended to harm me, but God intended it for good, to accomplish what is now being done, the saving of many lives."* (Genesis 50:20).

Repairing Broken Relationships

Submitted by Patty Mason

One day my husband and I were sitting at a car dealership finalizing a purchase transaction. As we sat there, the salesman, who was also the owner, told us about another man who cheated him. Angry, the salesman went on and on about what this man had done, and how he had hurt him. "How can I forgive this man?" The salesman questioned. "If I forgive him, it is like I am saying what he did was okay. And it's not okay."

Is Forgiveness an Ugly Word?

I can understand this line of thinking. There was a time I carried this same attitude. To me, forgiveness was an ugly word. Just like the car salesman, I thought forgiving someone who wronged me meant that what that person did was okay. The offense was okay. The abuse was okay. The betrayal was okay—but it wasn't okay.

A friend of mine suffered a heinous injustice when his 18 year old daughter was drugged and raped by a young man at a party. He was furious, so enraged by the boy's actions that he wanted to hunt him down and kill him.

I understand that when someone has wronged us, hurt us deeply, even hurt someone we love, it is hard not to take matters into our own hands and try to bring about vindication. It is human nature to want to lash out, to be angry, resentful, and full of unforgiveness. We want the person who hurt us, or hurt our loved one, to suffer. Somehow, this course of action justifies our suffering. But the truth of the matter is: Being unforgiving and vengeful only increases the pain.

The Hurt and Anger I Tried to Hide

For years I felt hurt and angry over the physical and emotional abuse I suffered as a child, but I never dealt with those harmful emotions. I tried to hide them, move forward and even pretend the abuse never happen; but, holding in all of that repressed hurt and anger was like standing beneath a volcano that was about to erupt. In order to find freedom from all of the hurt and pain from my past, I had to forgive. I had to forgive my dad, the kids at school and all the people who hurt me over the years.

The Day I Finally Forgave My Dad

I recall the day I finally forgave my dad. That morning, as I went about my day, the Holy Spirit brought a thought to mind: "Tell him you love him." At first, I wasn't sure who "he" was. No one in particular came to mind. Then, suddenly, as the thought, Tell him you love him, came to mind a second time, I thought of my dad.

Dad's reaction, the first time I told him I loved him, was not at all what I expected. He hugged me with tears in his eyes and told me he loved me, too. From that time on, he hugged me every chance he got. While growing up, I could count on one hand the number of times Dad hugged me—now he hugs me all the time. We talk, laugh, and share thoughts and conversations we never would have before.

Repairing Broken Relationships

I know what I am describing might sound too simple, maybe even impossible that a broken relationship could be repaired so quickly, but what I didn't realize until then was my dad was hurting too. He was no different than me. He was simply another wounded soul looking for love.

Before that day, I never took the time to get to know my father. I didn't realize all of what he had been through in his life—all of what he had suffered. After hearing his story, I understood my dad in a way I never understood him before. Suddenly, thought the power of the Holy Spirit, I was able to forgive him. Not because he deserved my forgiveness, or because it now gave me some kind of newfound power over him. Instead, forgiveness allowed me to open my heart.

Forgiveness is What Sets Us Free

Forgiving my dad didn't mean what he did was acceptable. It didn't right the wrong—I was still abused—but the abuse no longer had as much power over me. Exercising forgiveness allowed me to be set free from hate, resentment, anger and fear. Forgiveness gave me the opportunity to heal. Am I perfect? No, but with God's help I'm being restored. I'm in the process of finding deep, emotional healing from my past, and forgiving my dad was a huge step toward that healing.

And my friend whose daughter was raped, thankfully he sought the Lord instead of carrying out his threat. As a result, Christ helped Jim find forgiveness to where he began to pray for this young man. He even asked God to forgive this boy and to help him find redeeming grace. By the power of God's mercy, my friend was able to find it in his heart to exonerate that boy when at first it seemed impossible. Jim allowed Christ to work in his heart, and I allowed Him to work in mine.

Christ empowered us to forgive, just as God forgave a lost and dying world.

Forgiveness in the First Person

Submitted by Rita

I used to think at one time, that forgiveness was a two-way street – that when two individuals were at odds, they should come together to try and mend the scar that was created.

However, Jesus has been repeatedly confirming and reminding me through His Word, that forgiveness starts and ends…from within.

Everything Was Great in the Beginning

I was close friends with a colleague at work, what deepened our friendship was a mutual love for God's Word – the Bible. We would often share different Bible accounts, scriptures and faithful ones of the Bible. Because of this, we became inseparable while at work. This soon changed into communicating after work: calling, texting, emailing, and spending time together. We began to acknowledge each other as spiritual sisters.

The Tension Began

As time went on, we realized that there were some differences in what we were taught in our prospective spiritual upbringings. These differences began to slowly cause a strain in our friendship. I was told by her that I did not have a correct understanding of certain spiritual teachings.

This caused my friend to start correcting me and showing me literature, websites and other media that showed my spiritual beliefs in a very negative light. She also started becoming critical of me in other areas of my life. Needless to say, I did not respond to this in a positive way – actually, it hurt me very deeply.

Trying to Work Things Out

The first thing I brought to her attention was her comments on the other areas of my life. I felt the need to try and let her know how I felt about this. Her immediate reply was that she regretted trusting me and regretted that we had become friends. Her response floored me. I'm thinking, here I am trying to explain my thoughts and feelings to a friend and instead of acknowledging my feelings, it's 'I regret I trusted you'.

I decided to let things cool off, I sent an email acknowledging and apologizing for the hurt that I made her feel, as well as asking for her forgiveness – she never responded. A week went by – no email, no phone call, no communication of any kind.

When we were at work, she would walk by my work area and look forward. I will admit, the first thing that came to my mind is that we're supposed to be Christians first and foremost, and we're supposed to be friends and she's acting like this.

I took the time to apologize and ask for forgiveness, but I received nothing.

On one particular morning when she walked by my desk, I noticed that she seemed different, she didn't walk as fast as she had done previously, but again, she said nothing. I tried to make eye contact but she looked the other way. I checked my email about an hour after this and I saw a new email from her. I was surprised and delighted, thinking that this would be a renewed connection.

Instead, in the contents of the email from her, was a link to a video that disfavored my religious beliefs and showed them in a very negative light. I was angry and very upset and I voiced my extreme displeasure in an email to her immediately. I felt terrible for doing this, but at the same time, I wanted to let her know how deeply I was hurt by this last act on her part.

Again, she replied in a short, general statement, but no acknowledgement. Because of this, I decided to let her go and the friendship.

My Path to Healing

It's now been almost three weeks and, although there is no communication between us, I now realize that my communication with Christ should have been ongoing throughout this whole situation. However, it wasn't nearly as much as it should have been.

I began to think, 'What would Jesus have done?'....then I was quickly reminded that He already did it for me. With all the pain, suffering and torture that He went through, Jesus still prayed for those who hurt Him, and the actions they took against Him – He prayed for their forgiveness.

While I believe that one day, this individual and I may speak again, or maybe we won't, I have to make sure that within me, any feelings of pain, hurt and resentment are released.

Instead of continuing to expect or seek some form of acknowledgement or apology from her, I have to look to Jesus Christ for acknowledgement, and for whatever is lacking in me to be forgiving from the heart and to have peace within myself. This is really the only way – the best way – for me to heal and move on, no matter how much it hurts right now.

Forgiving My Dad and Accepting a New Family

Submitted by S'ambrosia Curtis

Losing my mother at the age of eighteen was undoubtedly the hardest situation I have yet faced. As her only daughter, we had a very special bond. I went everywhere she went, did everything she did, and talked to her about everything. Even when I made the mistake in high school of kissing a random boy in the park, I came right home and told her about it. I couldn't keep anything from her – She was my best friend.

Because of this solid foundation, I never once, during my mother's bout with cancer or after her death, turned my back on God. I had questions of course, but if anything, her death flung me deeper into the warmth of Christ's arms.

Still Grieving My Mother's Death

Two months after her passing, my dad began seeing another woman from our church. Shortly after that, he proposed to her without talking to us kids about it. Within eight months they were married, and I had a new stepmother who was younger than two of my siblings and two stepsisters that were accustomed to a different lifestyle than our own.

I Responded With Anger

With the traces of grief still ruminating in my heart, the sudden changes in my family almost felt like too much to deal with, so the path of response that I chose was one of anger. "How could he do this to us, and even worse, to Mom?" I made my anger known to my father, and all of my siblings shared my sentiment. No one was happy about this arrangement. Even most of the congregation of the church my dad pastored left the church in protest.

A Turning Point

This response continued until one day when my dad asked to take me to lunch as he was going to be in the city where I was attending college. I consented, but in the back of my mind I was planning all of the horrible things I would say to him. Nonetheless, I prayed before I left my dorm room and asked the Holy Spirit to give me a proper response. All I heard was that I was to be silent.

The tongue is truly a hard organ to control, but I submitted it to the direction of the Holy Spirit and managed to say nothing during my time with my father. After a few awkward pleasantries, my father began weeping in the middle of restaurant as he shared the pain he was dealing with, concerning everyone turning their back on him.

At that moment I realized that I had been so consumed with my own hurt and pain that I had not even stopped to think about what he was going through. My hard heart broke at seeing my dad in this state and I knew that regardless of how hard it was, I needed to forgive and love him as selflessly as I could.

Forgiveness and Sacrifice

That was about seven years ago, and since that meeting with my dad, the Lord has really taught me so much about forgiveness and sacrifice. Stepping outside of my desires, I am better able to see God's plan in all of this. My stepsisters desperately need Jesus, and it would be a shame for me to opt to wallow in self-pity and unforgiveness when I could be taking advantage of a God-given opportunity to show them His love and pray them into His kingdom. This marriage has nothing to do with me, but everything to do with them. It is my prayer that I never forget that.

Our Family is Still in the Process of Healing

Our family still has a long way to go before we're completely whole and healed, but after taking the first step of forgiveness, I have hope that He will be faithful to finish the good work that He started with us.

Sexual Abuse

Submitted by Tom Blubaugh.

When I was 12 years old, I was an altar boy for a hospital chaplain. Everyone trusted this priest and he was well known in the community. Little did they know he was sexually molesting me. I don't remember much of the details. My mind won't let me go there. I now know that I suppressed my feelings since I didn't know what to do with them. I didn't tell anyone about it until I was in my 40's.

At the age of 15, I was out of control and already a felon on probation. I was a pathological liar, but I kept myself out of reform school. I didn't know, until years later, that I was very angry and that my perception of God was twisted. Instead of seeing Him as a loving Father, I saw Him as a punitive God ready to punish me for every wrong thought and action.

I have gone through four bouts of devastating depression and in 1971 I went through an implosion while I was going through a divorce. I had horrible thoughts directed toward God that scared and tormented me. I didn't discover, until 2003, what that was about until I read "Anger: Handling a Powerful Emotion in a Healthy Way" by Gary Chapman. How God lead me to this book is a story of its own.

Over the four years that followed, God brought me the point of forgiveness–56 years after I was molested. I know I will never forget what was done to me, but I no longer hate the priest. I have given God my anger, resentment and hatred to take as far as the east is from the west.

Now, my relationship with my Father is healthier than ever and I no longer suppress anger. I am very grateful that the Lord kept me away from drugs and from taking my own life. He is good all the time.

Regret from the Past

Submitted by Nathan Buck

When I was a new believer, I had my first "Christian" dating relationship with someone that ended badly. I had met her through a Youth for Christ – Passion Play dinner theater that we were both a part of. She invited me to come to her church for a special music/worship time, and I went thinking this was an invitation to explore a dating relationship. The long story short is that it was initially just an invitation and that she was dating someone else. I however was persistent and interrupted that relationship.

We dated for about 6 months, and it was a roller-coaster of great God times and horribly selfish times. While we never crossed any major physical lines, the make-out sessions were in no way God honoring and we knew it. That fall I went to finish my last two years of college focused on preparing for ministry. God had called me to be a church planter, just before this relationship had started. As I sat in my dorm room one night wrestling with how God could want to use me for ministry when I couldn't even have a God honoring relationship, I was broken. I felt like I just kept repeating the same cycle over and over again in relationships.

In that moment God spoke clearly to me, and after reminding me of HIS call on my life, He said, "...if you want to know me more, then stop knowing her." I knew exactly what He meant, and I called her immediately (and excitedly I might add) to tell her God said we had to break up. She didn't share my excitement. My words hit her like a truck load of bricks and devastated her. She thought I had just found someone else at college. I never knew the depths of her pain and struggle till much later, but during that time, she went through counseling and dealt with a lot of issues that pre-dated our relationship. It was a very difficult journey for her. And I walked away carrying the disappointment I expected from her parents, her ex-boyfriend (who had become a good friend), and of course from her.

Flash forward a few years, and I get married to a wonderful woman who is a huge blessing to me. And I find out two days after our wedding this woman I had dated got married to her ex-boyfriend (they had grown a lot and God lead them forward to a great marriage).

Flash forward a few more years, and a mutual friend was getting married. We all would be there. It would be the first time we would all see each other since those painful days after the break-up. I was a mess, I could only feel the weight of disappointment, and expected to have to prove I had really grown up and changed. I found out later they too struggled with coming knowing I would be there.

We all ended up going, and when we walked in, Her husband looked at me with the same gleam of friendship in his eyes as in the past, and just said, "Hey" – as if no time had passed and we were picking up where we left off. That weekend was still emotionally difficult, but the moment of forgiveness that changed everything happened right after the wedding ceremony.

As we sat in the lobby, I told her husband how much I had been afraid to come, and how much I realized I missed his friendship most of all. Not that I didn't miss hers, but there was much in him as a friend that I admired and wanted to learn from. I shared how often I had seen in my mind, an image of disappointed stares from her and her parents and him. Mid-sentence He and she both stopped me, and said, "Nate, you have carried that far too long. As hard as it was for us, that is not a burden you should be carrying in your marriage. We bless you and forgive you in the name of Jesus, and we take away any disappointment on our behalf or her parents. You are forgiven and free to be who God wants you to be in your marriage and ministry!"

It was like years of rock and steel cages around my heart were melted, and I could breathe! It was the second most amazing time of forgiveness I had ever experienced. (The first was from my wife – and that's another story) After the reception, I cried the whole 5 hour drive home, and felt a continual sense of freedom growing in my heart.

Flash forward a few more years, and she and her husband were reading our updates about the church plant we had started, and felt lead by God to move their whole family to join us in ministry. They have become trusted friends, and their kids and our kids have grown together and continue to be best friends.

The Lord is good and His goodness and love will be brought to every situation submitted to Him (Romans 8:28-39).

Forgiving My Dad Who Abandoned Me

Submitted by Arthur Richardson

I was born in 1916 to two loving parents. Tragedy struck our home when I was just two and a half years old, and my mom suddenly died from a flu epidemic. A million people worldwide died from this epidemic. From what people tell me, my mother was a strong Christian and a very caring person.

Even though my dad tried his best to take care of us kids, it was very difficult. There were still many of us living at home and he ended up remarrying when I was just 4 or 5 years old. At first my stepmother tolerated me at home. However, as time went on, it was obvious that she viewed me as a nuisance and inconvenience in her life.

Out on the Streets

When I started school, she would tell me not to come home from school until my dad came home. I would walk the streets looking for something to do – It's a wonder I didn't get into more trouble! I see that as God's protection over my life.

Eventually my stepmother decided to leave my dad and take her kids with her. And instead of staying to be my provider and protector, my dad abandoned me to run after her. He left me and my other siblings, Albert and Beulah, by ourselves at home in order to be with her. And suddenly, I was without a mother or a father.

I Was Alone

When my dad didn't come back, we all had to find a way to survive. God provided loving foster parents for me, Glenn and India Topfer, that took me in. I also had brothers and sisters that loved me, but times were hard. We were in the middle of the depression and no one could afford to keep me. Therefore, my only choice was to be placed in an orphanage. I was just 12 years old and ended up spending a total of four years in the orphanage. I was an orphan – Abandoned and alone.

I Was Angry at My Dad

And for many years I was angry at my dad for leaving and abandoning us. What father would leave his children to take care of themselves? However, I was a hard worker and once I left the orphanage, I found work and was determined to make it on my own.

I was drafted into the army during World War II and when I returned after almost 57 months of service at the age of 25, my dad wanted me to work with him in construction. He offered to teach me the trade, but I wanted nothing to do with him. At that time, I was still too angry at him.

A Turning Point

However, just five years later – when I was around 30 years old – my dad was thrown off his horse and was in critical condition in the hospital. While receiving treatment in the hospital, he also became sick with pneumonia. On his death bed, my brother Albert and I were his only children to come and visit him. It was unbelievable to him that we were there – especially after all that he had done to us in the past.

We continued to visit him and one day my dad broke down and asked for our forgiveness. We could tell that his apology was sincere and in that moment, just a few days before his death, a healing occurred. Looking back, I see it as a miracle from God. This miracle, the miracle of forgiveness, restored my relationship with my dad.

Christ Came into My Life

Eventually, at the age of 31, I decided to get married to my beautiful wife, Lucille. Early in our marriage we both came to know Jesus as our Savior and began attending church. Christ made a difference in my life, and began to bring healing to my heart.

A Deeper Healing

A deeper healing and forgiveness happened in my heart, and I was finally able to forgive my dad. This lifted a load of anger, bitterness and resentment off of my shoulders as I was able to fully forgive my dad.

God has blessed me with a long life. As I share this story, I am 95 years old and have just celebrated my 64th wedding anniversary. My three daughters and their children all know the Lord. Many of my family are in full time ministry. I can only credit this to the work of Christ in my life. He came into my life and brought forgiveness, healing and new life. He adopted me into His family as His son. And for that I'm forever grateful.

Forgiveness is What Truly Sets Us Free

Submitted by Shelley Hitz

Two years ago, I was starting to feel distant from God and it seemed as if I couldn't sense His voice in my life as clearly in my life. So, I began to pray and asked God, "Is there something keeping me from hearing Your voice?"

I had remembered hearing someone say that if you're not hearing God's voice as clearly as you have in the past, ask yourself a question…"Is there something that God has asked me to do that I haven't done yet?" If so, He may be waiting for you to be obedient in what He's already asked you to do before He gives you something new.

So, I began to pray about this and realized that about six months before, I had sensed from God that I needed deeper healing in several relationships in my life. These relationships were with leaders in our church during a really difficult time when a major church split occurred. I had felt offended and hurt by some of their actions, some of their words and some of the things that happened.

God had brought me through the process of forgiving them. However, I realized that I also needed to ask them for forgiveness. Why? Well, you see, I had been judgmental of their actions. My sin was in judging them and holding bitterness in my heart for so long.

I felt strongly God leading me to contact these men who were leaders in our church at the time. I had put it off…for six months to be exact. I didn't want to do it, but God brought it to my mind again and I knew I needed to obey.

It's not as if I hear God's voice in an audible way, but I do sense His voice in my heart. I sense His Spirit leading and guiding me. The Bible says that His sheep hear His voice, (John 10:4) describing Jesus as the Shepherd and His followers as the sheep. If we have a relationship with Jesus, we will hear His voice in our lives.

As I began to realize that I needed to obey and do what God had already asked me to do, I prayed and asked God how I should contact these men. I didn't want to be inappropriate and I didn't necessarily want to show up out of nowhere knocking on their doors. Plus, some of them no longer lived in our town. Therefore, I felt God lead me to personally call them on the phone.

Do you know that within 24 hours I found all of their phone numbers and I was able to talk to each of them. Not only was it healing for me, but it was healing for them as well. I could tell that a couple of the men had tears in their eyes as I asked them for forgiveness. Then, as they responded by asking me for forgiveness for what they had done, it was an amazing experience. God truly brought healing and restoration through my step of obedience.

I wonder sometimes if there aren't more Christians like me, walking around with unresolved issues in their heart; i.e., unforgiveness, resentment or bitterness. Maybe you have felt God prompting you to go to a person and ask their forgiveness or to release that person in forgiveness and yet you don't want to do it. It's understandable. Like me, I didn't want to bring up the past and my old wounds. It felt hard. It felt difficult. It felt awkward. It felt unnecessary and, yet, God showed me that forgiveness is what truly sets us free and allows for a deeper healing and reconciliation to take place.

I'm wondering if there is anyone in your life that God is prompting you to approach and ask forgiveness or maybe to forgive them for something they have done to hurt you. I encourage you to ask God today and then to obey in whatever He asks you to do. It is worth it, even when the first step you take met with resistance. Ask God for strength today to obey Him in what He's asking you to do.

Seeking to Forgive Others

What about you? What is God asking you to do? Is there any unforgiveness, anger, resentment, hate or bitterness in your heart that you need to surrender to God?

If nothing comes to mind, pray and ask Him if there is something buried deep within your heart that you aren't even aware of right now. He may lead you on a path of healing and freedom you didn't even realize you needed.

Questions for Reflection

1. If you haven't done so already, I encourage you to start your own journal. You can do so in a simple notebook, a diary or other type of journal, or on your computer.

2. I encourage you to start with prayer. You might want to pray a prayer of surrender. If so, you can pray something like this,

   Lord, I want to be free from anything that weighs me down and the sin that so easily entangles. (Heb 12:1-2). I surrender to you my heart, mind and will and ask that you lead me through this time of journaling and prayer. Help me to be willing to deal with the issues of my past that are hindering my spiritual growth. I acknowledge your power to overcome sin and to help me do what I cannot do myself. Amen.

3. In your journal, write out any people you may be holding unforgiveness, anger, resentment, hate or bitterness in your heart against. If nothing comes to mind, pray and ask God if there is something buried deep within your heart that you aren't even aware of right now.

4. Journal about the experience and why it made you angry or hurt you. One thing that has helped me in the past is to write a fictitious letter to the person who has hurt or offended me.

   If the experience is especially painful, you may want to talk with a counselor, pastor or close friend instead.

5. Pray and ask God what other steps you should take to be able to "forgive from your heart."

6. Once you are ready, you can pray a prayer of forgiveness.

   There is no "magic prayer" but you can choose to use the following prayer as an example. Enter the person's name in the blanks below.

   Lord, I confess and repent of my sin of holding unforgiveness against _____ for the ways they have hurt me and of my anger and resentment against You, God, for allowing this to happen in my life.

   I ask You to forgive me, and I receive Your forgiveness. I forgive myself for participating in this sin.

   I am now ready to offer forgiveness to _____ for the ways they have hurt me. I ask for the empowerment of the Holy Spirit to help me truly forgive _____ from my heart. Right now, I visualize a backpack of weight on my shoulders, the weight of unforgiveness. It is so heavy. I now choose to take it off of my shoulders and give it to you. I let go of it and let it drop into your hands. I trust you to bring justice for situation and any wrong that has been done. Thank you for taking this weight from me. Amen.

Part Two:

Asking God's Forgiveness

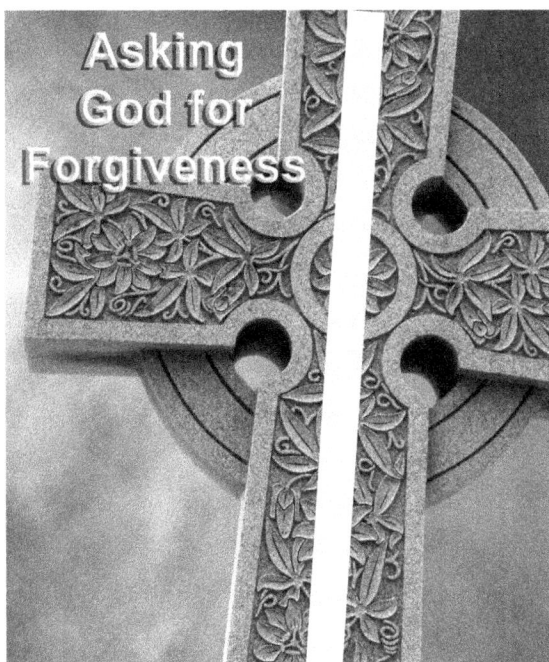

Asking
God for
Forgiveness

My Abortion:
A Prisoner's Lesson in Forgiveness

Submitted by Christina Ryan Claypool

An Excerpt from her book,

Forgiven: finding peace in the aftermath of abortion

Trapped in a crisis pregnancy, alone and afraid, I made a tragic choice to end the life of my own child. For years, I was unable to forgive myself for having had an abortion on Dec. 3, 1983.

I knew that I was a "murderer," and despite becoming a Christian believer in 1986, I could never seem to accept God's forgiveness for what I had done.

That is until I met a man who I will refer to as "Sam," a prisoner convicted of taking the life of my high school friend, "Ben." This meeting occurred in the late 1990's when I was a Christian television reporter, reluctantly sent into the prison to interview him to warn young people about the dangers of drugs and alcohol.

Sam didn't know that Ben had been my friend when he agreed to let me interview him. When I met Sam, he wasn't at all what I had expected. He was a very intelligent man who was extremely honest. As I asked the questions that I had prepared for the interview, his answers came automatically. He was not trying to impress anyone, but he was trying to be accurate.

For about an hour, Sam presented the events that led up to Ben's death, including his own troubled adolescence plagued by alcohol and drug use. His desire to be a tough guy, but being afraid – afraid that somebody would find out that inside he wasn't really that tough.

The alcohol and drug addiction escalated to a night when he was in, what he described as, a "rough and tumble kind of bar" where he started to fight with Ben. Ben humiliated him, and Sam's fragile pride couldn't take that. He went home found a gun, came back and emptied the chamber of the gun into Ben's body. He didn't even remember pulling the trigger that night because he was too high on drugs and alcohol, but he did remember standing over Ben's collapsed form with the gun in his hand.

He said he hadn't minded being labeled a murderer so much when he was young. It brought a kind of fear to other prisoners, giving him some protection. Although, the stigma of being labeled a murderer really began to bother him as he grew older. "You can't be labeled anything worse," he said candidly.

Sam didn't know how well I understood the heavy burden of being a convicted murderer. I hadn't been convicted by society; they had even sanctioned my crime. Yet, once I came to know Christ's commandments, I knew that I, too, had taken an innocent life. I wanted to tell Sam that I understood, and that we shared the same label, but I couldn't since the warden's assistant stood along the wall guarding our conversation.

I waited for him to blame Ben for being a bully; instead he accepted accountability for his crime. Saying, "I think today of what I altered. The children that were never born, the birthday parties that man will never attend." Sam confessed that what he took away, that was probably the greatest loss, was life itself. "As long as there's life there is hope," he added remorsefully. I was reminded of the Scripture in Ecclesiastes 9:4, "Anyone who is among the living has hope..."

My thoughts went to the child I had aborted; who I believed was a baby girl – the daughter I would never have. She would never experience the thrill of a first date or attend a High School prom. There would be no pretty white dress and veil for her wedding day, or the opportunity to have children. I had removed the hope of life in a matter of seconds on an abortionist's table. Sam had stolen those same things from Ben and his family, and he couldn't change the past anymore than I could.

Something in me broke at that moment. Somehow, my enemy had become my friend, because we were both murderers in desperate need of God's forgiveness. Sam said that it had almost driven him insane trying to deal with the guilt of what he'd done, "How could he pay for his crime?" he asked. "With his life, with life in prison, what was the right punishment?"

I vividly saw myself in his words. Year after year, I grieved and couldn't be consoled, because I was too ashamed to tell anyone I needed help. I had given myself a life sentence, too, but until I met Sam I didn't have a hope for parole.

God healed something inside of me that day in the prison that far exceeded any bitterness I held towards Sam. God showed me a man who had the courage to tell the whole truth in the hope that it might help others. For the first time, I fully understood God's gift of forgiveness extended to another, and I knew that same gift was available to me, no matter what.

The Forgiveness Verse

Submitted by Scott Mason

There's one verse in the Bible that I believe everyone should know without exception, and that is 1 John 1:9. The forgiveness verse, as I call it, states that: *"If we confess our sins, He is faithful and just and will forgive us our sins and purify us from all unrighteousness."*

There's one word that stands out to me more than any other word in that verse, and it is purify. The definition of purify is to rid of impurities – to cleanse. What John is saying here is that God will not only forgive our sins, but He will also purify, cleanse and restore us to the state we were in before our sin – our original state.

When Shelley Hitz asked me to write a story on forgiveness for her blog and book, "Unshackled and Free: True Stories of Forgiveness," it took about 10 seconds to figure out what I was going to write on. I could've talked about how God has forgiven me of my past life which consisted of being addicted to drugs and alcohol, arrested over 25 times, 36 felony convictions, and 10 years in prison, but that's not what God wanted.

God wanted me to share how I use the verse in 1st John to help prostitutes, sex addicts and anyone who has had sex outside of marriage. Below is one story that took place in October of 2010, and it is similar to every other person I do this with. I hope it helps you find forgiveness in your own life if you have had sex outside of God's will.

Sometimes You Have to Head Straight into the Pain to Come Out on the Other Side

One afternoon I met with up with a girl who, at the time, was addicted to almost any drug she could put into her veins. In order to pay for the drugs she was addicted to, she would sleep with countless men. At one point she was having sex with over 30 people a day. As we started to talk about her lifestyle I noticed right away that the sex she was having to support her habit really weighed heavy on her heart. Now, you would think that something like this would bother just about anyone, but when you're living in sin it just becomes second nature.

So I asked her, "Why, out of all the stuff that you do to support your drug habit, is this one that bothers you the most?" Her response shocked me. She talked about how she knew that one day God would deliver her from her habit and that once that happened, she wanted to have a husband and children like she used to dream about when she was growing up. She went on to talk about how no man in their right mind would ever want to marry her because of her sexual past and this is what was weighing so heavily on her. She asked me, "Do you think any godly man would want me?"

Before I answered her question, I went back into my office and grabbed a devotional that a friend of mine written and my Bible. I sat back down and said, "Before I answer your question I want you to follow me on this. This devotion I have in my hand is called 'Hope for Lily.' Lily means purity. I would give you this devotional, but it really wouldn't mean too much to you. You have slept with so many men that it would just be a waste of time for you to read it." She sat there in that chair with tears running down her face. Any hope that she had, I had just ripped it from her in a few sentences. "But I do have something I want to share with you," I told her. I opened my Bible up to 1 John 1:9, and I asked her to read it. She read it out loud with trembling in her voice. "If we confess our sins, He is faithful and just and will forgive us our sins and purify us from all unrighteousness." I said, "do you realize what this means? It means that if you confess your sexual sins and turn from them, that God will not only forgive you, but also purify you back to the original state that He intended for you to be. That state is being a virgin until you are married.

Well, something must have clicked inside of her, because her tears went from sadness to joy, and in between her crying she asked God to forgive her of all her sins, including the sexual ones, and then proclaimed: "I am once again a virgin." I sat there and looked at her for a moment with joy in my heart, like a proud father looks at his children, and slid the devotional across the table to her and said, "This devotional now has everything to do with you. You are now pure, you are now a virgin. ...Oh yeah, and by the way, yes I believe that a godly man would want to share his life with you."

Forgiven and Free

Today, that girl is serving Jesus, has been off of drugs for quite a long time, and has been saving herself for marriage. She tells anyone and everyone she can, that she is a virgin – even though she was once a hooker. How awesome is that?

Seeking God's Forgiveness

Are you ready to change directions in your life? If, so let God know. Confess the ways you've been going down the wrong path. Use Psalm 51 as your prayer if you don't know how to start.

And then ask God to empower you with His Holy Spirit to change directions. You may have to make some hard choices. I know I did. It was not easy. But, God gave me the strength to obey. And He will give you what you need as well.

And, guess what?

You'll find true life on the other side. And you'll realize that Jesus' teachings really do add up to a full life.

Questions for Reflection:

1. I encourage you to start with prayer. You might want to pray a prayer of surrender. If so, you can pray something like this,

   Lord, I want to be free from anything that weighs me down and the sin that so easily entangles. (Hebrews 12:1-2). I surrender to you my heart, mind and will and ask that you lead me through this time of journaling and prayer.

   Help me to be willing to deal with any sin in my life that keeps me from you and hinders my spiritual growth. I acknowledge your power to forgive any sin and to help me do what I cannot do myself. Amen.

2. In your journal, write out any current sin in your life that comes to mind. It could be an outward sin like getting drunk at parties or it could be an inward sin like jealousy or pride. If nothing comes to mind, pray and ask God to reveal to you any sin that is coming between you and Him.

3. Once you are ready, you can pray a prayer asking God for forgiveness of your sins. There is no "magic prayer" but you can choose to use the following prayer as an example.

Lord, I confess and repent of my sin (s) of _____ and of my anger and resentment against You, God, for allowing this to happen in my life. I ask You to forgive me, and I receive Your forgiveness. I forgive myself for participating in this sin.

I ask for the empowerment of the Holy Spirit to help me truly repent of my sin(s) of _____ and help me to change directions. Please show me how I need to change and help me through the Holy Spirit to make those changes despite what my friends and family may think or say. Thank you for taking the weight of this sin from me and restoring my relationship with You. Amen.

4. Write out any changes you sense God asking you to make as you repent of your sin (s). I recommend that you find an accountability partner to help you and pray for you as you make these changes.

Part Three:
Forgiving Yourself

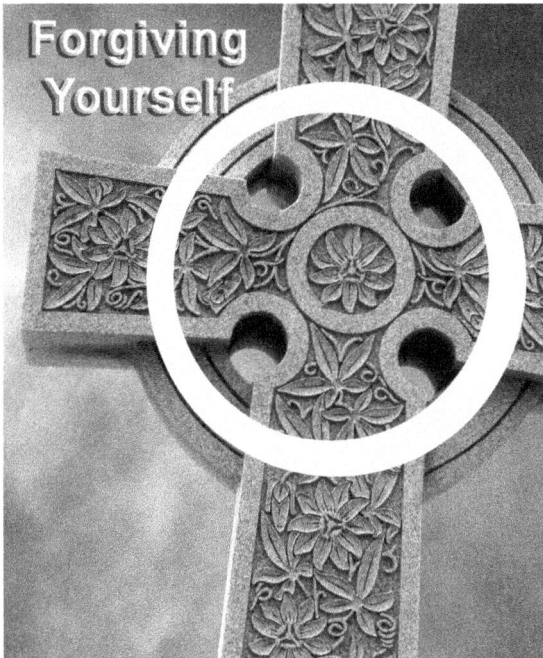

Forgiving Myself Set Me Free

Submitted by Julie Lambie

I remember waking up one day and thinking, "Wow my world has fallen apart!" I was dizzy, confused, sick, anxious and starting having panic attacks. What I didn't know was why. I spoke to a beautiful trusted friend who I had been spending time with who was like a spiritual mother. She showed me that my negativity and anger towards what I thought was other people was truly at myself.

I was bitter, angry, hurt and resentful inwardly but outwardly smiled like life was awesome and I was in control, but the day my world fell apart it also opened up into the most painful but rewarding season of healing I have ever experienced. My story is one of truth. Jesus said in John 8.32, "Then you will know the truth...and the truth will set you free."

You see, when you live your life in lies and pretense nothing good can last and nothing good can come out of it. I started to be honest with myself about who I was and not who I thought I believed I was, I also started believing that I was worthy and able and had something to offer - not just myself but my family and even others.

I started to forgive myself on such an intimate level it changed me and allowed me to see others differently as well.

I'm still on this journey where God has taken me into a deeper place as forgiveness. To me it didn't just start and end - it was and is a journey - an amazing journey where healing and change enabled me to be me. I can now see that I truly love and accept that being me is perfect for me.

Forgiving Myself for Being Angry at God

Submitted by Saundra-Dalton Smith

I love God, but loving God did not prevent me from becoming mad at Him. As I young girl I've always known my home situation was different.

My parents were a young couple when I was conceived. My dad was in the military and my mom was in college. Had life turned out the way they had planned it, they would have entered the hospital in March 1973 as two and left as three. Unfortunately that was not God's plan.

For unknown reasons, my mother started having medical difficulty soon after child birth. What should have been a joyous event turned into a season of deep mourning. My 26 year old military dad walked to the hospital a husband and left a widow with a newborn baby girl.

He was completely unprepared to care for an infant alone, so in stepped my great-grandmother. At 77 years old she was still the matriarch of the family and the one whose faith could move mountains. This turn of events didn't seem to catch her off guard. She was well rooted in her relationship with God and had long ago learned the power of trusting him.

Being raised in this atmosphere of deep faith however did not prevent the inevitable; a personal feeling that some way God had let me down. Why did my mother have to die? Why could my home life not be like everyone else I knew? How am I to trust a God who would allow such a horrible thing to happen? I had a lot of questions for God and I believed I deserved an answer, but no answers came. I spent many nights of crying myself to sleep as a girl and later a young adult. Hours of daydreaming about the what if's and the if only's of life. Every time I would pray for some type of heavenly sign, some type of answer to explain away the pain. But no answers came and each time I would leave those moments crestfallen and heartbroken; angry and upset at God.

I decided if God was not trustworthy to handle something as basic as childbirth, then He was not worth to handle my life and my destiny. I was sure I could do a much better job at taking care of my affairs, so I made my life plan and went after it. Despite my rebellion, God was gracious and blessed my efforts. Smiling down on me and loving me through the days of my self-sufficient idolatry. He allowed me to bloom in spite of the thorns that were pricking my heart, but the thorns over time started to suffocate my spiritual and personal growth. The thorns of anger and bitterness I held towards God eventually started to strangle my ability to grow into the woman He had created me to be.

On the brink of one of my greatest life decisions, God allowed me to see a part of His heart towards me. I had reached a place of desperately wanting to know Him more and to understand my past pain. In those moments He spoke to my heart "Do you trust me?"

I then recalled all of the many blessings He had showered down on me. In the middle of my bitterness and anger, God had never stopped loving me. In my inability to let go of the pain, I had developed a distorted view of God and His role in my life. God didn't need my forgiveness, after all He is God. However, I needed to forgive myself for my anger and allow God to heal my distorted view of Him. It was the only way I would ever move on and start developing a new level of intimacy with Him.

***

Regardless of whatever painful events have happened in your life, God understand your anger. He will even allow you grace to express that anger and vent your frustration; He's big enough to handle it. But there will also come a time when you must let go of the pain, forgive, and move forward. It is the only way to full rest in His faithfulness, goodness, and loving-kindness towards you.

Forgiven

Submitted by Kimberley Payne

I flopped in my chair, "You want me to do what?"

'Forgive,' the voice in my head replied.

"You've got to be kidding. Forgiveness needs to be deserved."

'If that were true, my death on the cross would be for naught.'

I looked out the living room window. A small black bird dive bombed a red-tailed hawk. The sun shone bright against a watery blue sky but the air betrayed the winter chill. I pulled a quilt over my lap. "True. But I would have to forget. To forgive and forget."

'Another fallacy. Although I have the ability to remove transgressions as far as the east is from the west, you do not. But when you choose to forgive, the memory loses its sting. It won't be forgotten but the pain of remembering will no longer be there.'

"But if I forgive, everyone may think that I don't feel it was a huge offense. It'll look like I don't think it matters. Like I condone it." I played with the edges of the blanket. Blue-Kasey, my Russian Blue cat, jumped up, circled once and settled on my lap.

'What's more important to you – men or Me?'

My chin sagged to my chest. "You, of course." I made patterns in Blue-Kasey's silver-blue fur with my finger. "But doesn't forgiving excuse the person for doing wrong?"

'It doesn't excuse them, but it does release you. It releases you from the anger and resentment of unforgiveness.'

"I remember someone saying that not forgiving is like trying to get back at someone else by drinking poison. I suppose it does me no good to hold onto unforgiveness."

'Yes, forgiveness frees the forgiver. You want freedom don't you?'

"Yes! I'm tired of carrying this burden. My shoulders feel so heavy. I haven't laughed in months. I need to release it."

'Forgive.'

"I can't do it on my own."

'I'll help you.'

"Okay. With Your help, I can do this. I choose to forgive. I choose to be free." I picked up Blue-Kasey, kissed him between his furry ears, stood up and walked down the hall. Taking a deep breath, I slowly opened the bedroom door. I stepped in. I looked into the beveled mirror. My reflection, tentative but determined, stared back.

"I forgive you."

The face in the mirror smiled.

'Good child. Forgive others, including yourself, as you have been forgiven.'

Losing My Virginity

Submitted by Tabea

When I was 18, I had a boyfriend for two and a half years who did not believe in Jesus. For a long time this wasn't a problem for me because we liked to do the same things and had a lot of fun together. Also we often had the same point of view in important matters. He always accepted my belief and we had many good talks about God and my life as His child, but he never wanted to go to church with me. He was always interested, but skeptic at the same time. He never wanted to take a look at my church or Bible study group. Now I know that the relationship with him caused me to drift away from my Father in Heaven. During the relationship I didn't realized that, nor did I want to.

I don't know. But one day we had sex... and not only one time. However, after a few months, I suddenly realized that I could not continue doing this because it didn't feel right. My relationship with my Heavenly Father was in pieces, and that made me indescribably sad. So I prayed, and talked with my boyfriend about that, and from that day on we no longer had sex anymore.

But I felt that I did not live in God's will completely. So after many months of inner conflicts and crying I decided to break up with my boyfriend. This wasn't an easy decision. I always wanted sex with only one guy in my life, preferably with my husband. But now I had sex with him, and I was so sad about that fact because I thought that no one would ever love me again. I had given away the precious gift of my virginity. What could I give my future husband?!

I was hopeless. For a long time I didn't want to see or talk to anybody; I only wanted to be alone. But then God spoke to me clearer than He ever had before. He told me that He loves me, no matter what I've done and that He had forgiven me a long time ago. He said that I always was His beautiful princess and that He wants to restore my heart. He wanted to restore everything inside of me, all that was broken and hurt, and He wants to wash me clean and white and pure as snow. He also told me that He has a wonderful husband for me, who will love me like He does and who will forgive me that I cannot give him the gift of my virginity.

My Heavenly Father sent me people who listened to my story and feelings and who prayed for me. From that day on I felt everyday more and more God's grace and love for me. And today I know that He has forgiven me completely, and I know that He has an awesome plan for my life. Somewhere in this world there is a man who will love me and forgive me all of my faults which I have made in past relationships with guys. I praise God that He has made me free, and helped me so that I could forgive myself and live now a life in His grace.

Forgiving Myself
Submitted by Deidre Hall

When I entered high school as a freshman I started dating a guy who was two years older than I was. Although he claimed to a Christian, he was very caught up in what the world was doing. He wanted to do a lot of physical things in our relationship, and I wasn't strong enough to say "no." So we crossed a lot of boundaries, to the point of almost having sex.

Eventually the relationship ended, but the guilt didn't. I never got caught by my parents or punished at all for what happened, so I decided to punish myself. I told myself that it was my fault that things got that far and that I should have known better. I was placing the cloud of guilt over my head, allowing it to follow me wherever I went.

What I didn't realize was I was placing myself above God. God had forgiven me! Me not forgiving myself was telling God that Jesus dying for me on the cross wasn't enough. I had forgiven the guy, but made myself regret those things for years. I was listening to Shelley give one of her presentations on forgiveness when I realized I had to forgive myself. Jesus loved me enough to die for me, and no matter what I did, He forgave me and loved me all the more. So I put those things behind me and no longer walk with an inner guilt.

I'm forgiven!

My Unforgiveness and How I Punished Myself

Submitted by LaToya Gay

I never realized how much unforgiveness I had stored in my heart until one day I just broke down crying. All of the memories and every negative thing that could've happened to me surfaced including all the bitterness, envy, and hatred that I had ever felt towards my uncle who had tried to molest me twice at the age of 11 and 12.

How I Punished Myself

For years, I punished myself by sleeping around with men, smoking, drinking, and whatever else I could think of to suppress my pain. You see, my dad refused to take my side on that day when I told him what my uncle had tried to do to me. He just wrote it off and said that they were all drinking and he probably did not mean to do it.

Recovering From the Pain

God really had to do a work in me, and He is still helping me recover from the pain and suffering that I went through in my younger days. Before I allowed God to heal my heart, He told me to get in His Word and pray, and He brought my attention to a scripture, which was Ephesians 4:32, ESV, *"Be kind to one another, tenderhearted, forgiving one another, as God in Christ forgave you."*

He pointed out to me that I needed to forgive myself before I could go on the journey of forgiving others. I am still working on that. It is a battle that I continue to fight, and I encourage those who are struggling with forgiveness to learn how to love yourselves, learn how to forgive yourselves, and God will help you forgive others.

Forgiving Yourself:
A Necessary Step to Overcoming Guilt
Submitted by Michael Okyere Asante

One day in school, a colleague asked me to accompany her so she could visit a friend who had been admitted at a nearby hospital. When we got there, her friend had been discharged and was being helped to pack his things. In that same room was another patient who looked familiar but was difficult to make out.

The Holy Spirit told me it was a friend I knew and asked me to lay hands on him. I couldn't believe what I was hearing because I had seen that friend two weeks before. I couldn't believe it was him lying on the bed so sick, pale and thin. I hesitated and decided to say a word of prayer in my mind for him.

A Missed Opportunity

Two days later, I heard that this patient had died and I also got to know that the friend I had seen two weeks before was the same patient I couldn't make out at the hospital. I couldn't take it—I was overwhelmed with grief and I cried throughout the night. Even though I had asked God to forgive me, for weeks I was downhearted and guilt-ridden.

God took away my burden when I was able to finally forgive myself and accept His forgiveness.

Loaded Down With Guilt

Many times, after turning away from God, we become guilt-ridden; we consider ourselves not worthy of God's grace. Like the Prodigal Son we tell God, *"I am no longer worthy to be called your son; make me like one of your hired men"* (Luke 15:19). But no matter what we have done, God still loves us and is willing to receive us (Isa. 1:18).

In Luke 15 the Prodigal Son came to his senses, but because of his guilt he had already pronounced judgment on himself: his father will not forgive him; the best he will do is to make him as one of the hired men (Luke 15:19). But the Bible says that when the lost son *"was still a long way off, his father saw him and was filled with compassion for him"* (Luke 15:20a). He didn't end there; *"he ran to his son, threw his arms around him and kissed him."* Luke 15:20b.

The Love of a Father

It didn't matter the things his son had wasted in his life; it didn't matter the filthiness of his garment nor the stench it emitted; he threw his arms around his son and kissed him. What a loving father! The lost son confessed that he was unworthy to be called his son (Luke 15:19), but that wasn't important to the father; what mattered was that his son had returned to him. He ordered the servants to clothe him and a royal welcome party was thrown for his return.

What is Your Situation?

Is it just like mine, like that of the Prodigal Son, better than it or even worse? How far have you ran from God? How rebellious have you been? How long have you closed your ears to His calling? It is never too late to return to the Lord. If guilt is preventing you, then you haven't forgiven yourself. If you do not forgive yourself, it will be difficult to accept another person's forgiveness, and you will be giving the devil further foothold in your life. One ancient writer said, "The cruel person is fed, not broken, by (another's) tears."

God's Forgiveness

Paul trusted in God's forgiveness in spite of his blasphemy against God, and persecution and violence against Christians (1 Tim. 1:13). In Philippians 3:13, 14 he says, *"Forgetting what is behind and straining toward what is ahead, I press on toward the goal to win the prize for which God has called me heavenward in Christ Jesus."*

Can you also trust God to forgive you? God forgave me. He will also forgive you!

Sexual and Emotional Abuse

Submitted by Kimberly James

Forgiveness – I think we all underestimate its significance. We think of it as a nice gesture to extend to someone who may have done us wrong in some capacity. While that is true, the biggest piece of it is related to the connection between your capacity to forgive others as the "portal" to being able to receive forgiveness from ourselves and from God.

I had to learn the hard way that forgiveness is not for them as much as it is for us. Personally, I never realized that my capacity to love and receive love from others and from God Himself was being blocked by a spirit of unforgiveness. I was bitter, angry and vengeful for a long time and I didn't like myself very much. Why?

I will be 40 years old in January of 2012 and it took the past four years of debilitating trials, in every area of my life, to force me to deal with the shackles that have held me back my entire life.

As a child, I was sexually and emotionally abused for 14 years. I was an adult before I ever told anyone about it, but unfortunately that was years after I had been raped multiple times in my teen and young adult years. I blamed myself for everything that had happened to me, because I was known to be promiscuous. In each situation, I was either drunk, or high, or both, and likely some place I wasn't supposed to be, so I used how people (especially men) hurt me as an excuse for my bitterness and treatment of others.

BUT GOD... took me back to the time and place where I was first violated, which created the thought in my mind that I deserved what happened to me, and allowed me to feel unworthy of love, acceptance (as I was – even wounded) and forgiveness. Those thoughts ultimately made me feel that it was ok for people to hurt me, because "I deserved it," thus putting myself in vulnerable situations and surrounding myself with untrustworthy people.

It was a very painful process to wholeness, focusing heavily on my need to forgive those who abused me, as well as those who I felt didn't protect me, but mostly being able to forgive myself for the bad choices that I made in my state of pain and confusion. Of course at the time, you don't make the connection between the things that happened that were out of your control and the things that were, but in hind sight I am grateful for God carrying me through all of those experiences to allow me to minister to others with similar backgrounds and challenges.

I know now that forgiveness is what sets you free from whatever it is that keeps you connected to whomever hurt you – sometimes, that unhealthy soul tie is within ourselves, and that's what the enemy wants... He wants us to secretly wallow in guilt and shame to keep us from our destiny and accomplishing our purpose.

You can't forgive yourself in a world that thrives on judgment and guilt, unless you can bypass the middle man and build a relationship with God Himself that is not based on the standards or examples of earthly love; because life has given us all a warped perception of what truly unconditional love is.

Once I achieved that by letting God's love replace the understanding of love that I formed, based on the father who abandoned me and the men who abused me while telling me they loved me more than anything in this world, then I had a clean slate to build upon. I was finally able to receive God's unconditional love and forgiveness, thus allowing me to forgive myself and to extend it to others.

Once you get that down, the rest comes much easier because you stop interpreting everything that goes wrong in your life through a victim mentality. We were not made to be victims; we were made to be victors!

Reverse Polarity

Submitted by CJ Hitz

I know, I know. Reverse polarity...what's that? I wasn't familiar with those words either, at least when they're used together. I am now.

A few weeks ago Shelley & I came out of Panera Bread in Lancaster, PA, and prepared to leave when our Toyota RV wouldn't start. Completely dead, not a peep when I turned the key. Fortunately, we also had our car with us which Shelley was driving.

"We'll just use the car to jumpstart the RV battery," I confidently told my wife.

I proceeded to put the cables on each of the batteries, looking to make sure the black cables were placed on the negative terminals and the red cables carefully placed on the positive terminals.

I should have gotten the hint when sparks flew upon attaching the cables to the RV battery but after a second or two, the sparks ceased. Seeing a black cover on one of the RV battery terminals, I assumed that was the negative. The other terminal didn't have any cover. Did I mention it was 10:00 pm, rainy, and dark outside?

"Go ahead and start the car, Shelley."

We let the car run for 30 minutes and prayed before attempting to start the RV again. Nothing. Zilch. Dead.

"Maybe we need new jumper cables," I said, trying to sound like a man with a 'sure fire' back up plan.

Unfortunately, we just missed getting into the Wal-Mart next door before they closed. So we'd have to sleep in the Panera parking lot until they opened the next morning.

We awoke the next morning and grabbed some fresh Panera coffee and bagels before heading into Wal-Mart for those brand new cables which would surely do the trick. Again, I placed the cables on each battery as I had the night before…yes, some sparks flew. Hint not taken.

"Go ahead and start the car Shelley."

We let the car run for 30 minutes and prayed before attempting to start the RV again. I slowly turned the key while pushing on the gas…

Crickets.

"That must be one dead battery," I said. We decided upon a local towing company who also happened to have some excellent mechanical skills. They took the RV back to their shop and, upon inspection, we indeed realized the cables were backward on the RV battery. This is also referred to as…

Reverse Polarity.

Google these words and you'll see anything from minor damage to your electrical system to frying the whole system and more. After looking everything over, the mechanics determined we were somewhere in the middle. We basically fried the alternator and needed it replaced along with some fuses.

The Worst Damage...

...occurred as I beat myself up over and over again in my mind for the next 24 hours. Isn't the damage we inflict upon ourselves always some of the worst? Especially for those of us who have a tendency toward perfectionism.

Some of the thoughts I was chewing on included...

"You idiot, you can't even jumpstart your own car correctly!"
"Because of my stupid mistake, we're out $350 more than we should be."
"We could be on the road to Florida by now, but you screwed that up, CJ!"
"Just another failure in a long line of them, huh?"
"Maybe this whole 'living in an RV' thing was a dumb idea."

You can see how things could continue to spiral downward in a hurry. Thankfully, the Lord broke through and rescued me from that "stinkin' thinkin'." These thoughts aren't the sum total of CJ Hitz but choosing to believe them put me into a temporary prison.

With the help of my wonderful wife, I was able to forgive myself for this costly blunder and move on. When you're able to look back and get a good laugh, it's a sign you've been able to let it go. In fact, I think Jesus got a chuckle out of the whole thing from the beginning. He was never mad at me for royally screwing up. It was simply a learning experience. A chance to let good triumph over evil within my mind.

And what else did you learn, CJ?

Confusing the positive with the negative can certainly create sparks.

"And now, dear brothers and sisters, one final thing. Fix your thoughts on what is true, and honorable, and right, and pure, and lovely, and admirable. Think about things that are excellent and worthy of praise."

~Philippians 4:8, NLT

Seeking to Forgive Yourself

Forgiving yourself is one of the most overlooked parts of the forgiveness cross. And yet, it's often an important and crucial part of our healing process. Jesus wants to enter the areas of brokenness in your heart and bring healing and restoration.

Questions for Reflection:

1. I encourage you to stop right now and pray. Ask God to come into any brokenness that remains in your heart and bring healing. He will empower you and help you let go of your past and forgive yourself so that you can embrace your future.

2. You might want to pray a prayer of surrender. If so, you can pray something like this,

   Lord, I desire to be free from anything that weighs me down and the sin that so easily entangles. (Hebrews 12:1-2). I surrender to you my heart, mind and will and ask that you lead me through this time of journaling and prayer. Help me as I bring my brokenness to you and my regret, shame and failures of the past. I acknowledge your power to heal the brokenhearted and forgive <u>all</u> unrighteousness. Come now and help me do what I cannot do myself. Amen.

3. In your journal, write out any regret, shame or failure from your past that comes to mind. If nothing comes to mind, pray and ask God to reveal any area of brokenness in your heart that needs His healing touch.

4. Once you are ready, you can pray a prayer asking God for forgiveness of your sins and to also forgive yourself for

your mistakes of the past. There is no "magic prayer" but you can choose to use the following prayer as an example.

Lord, I confess and repent of my sin(s) of _____and of my anger and resentment against You, God, for allowing this to happen in my life. I ask You to forgive me, and I receive Your forgiveness.

I forgive myself for participating in this sin.

I ask for the empowerment of the Holy Spirit to help me truly repent of my sin(s) of _____ and help me to change directions. Please show me how I need to change and help me through the Holy Spirit to make those changes despite what my friends and family may think or say. Thank you for taking the weight of this sin and brokenness from me and restoring my relationship with You. Amen.

Jesus has come to *bind up the brokenhearted, to proclaim freedom for the captives and release from darkness for the prisoners. (Isaiah 61:1)*

In Conclusion: The Forgiveness Cross

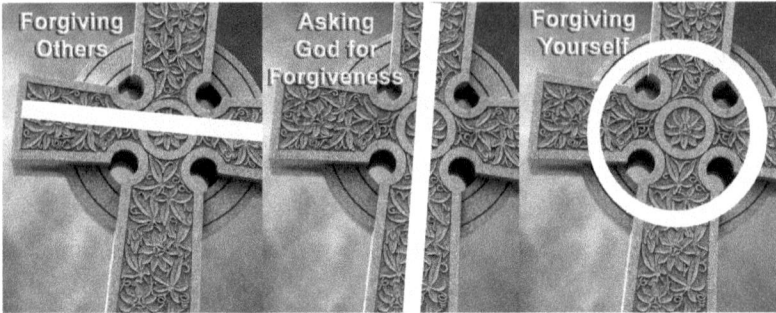

1. Forgiving Others
2. Asking God for Forgiveness
3. Forgiving Yourself

We pray that you will ***never forget*** the illustration of the forgiveness cross. Then, when you need it, God can bring it to the forefront of your mind over and over as He has done in ours.

Forgiveness is truly what sets you free...*there is power in forgiveness!*

Appendix One: Forgiveness Scriptures

Forgiving Others

Matthew 6:14-15
"For if you forgive men when they sin against you, your heavenly Father will also forgive you. But if you do not forgive men their sins, your Father will not forgive your sins." (NIV)

Mark 11:25-26
"If you have anything against anyone, forgive him and let it drop (leave it, let it go) in order that your Father who is in heaven may also forgive you your [own] failings and shortcomings and let them drop. But if you do not forgive, neither will your Father in heaven forgive your failings and shortcomings" (AMP)

Matthew 18:15-17
"If your brother wrongs you, go and show him his fault, between you and him privately. If he listens to you, you have won back your brother. But if he does not listen, take along with you one or two others, so that every word may be confirmed and upheld by the testimony of two or three witnesses. If he pays no attention to them [refusing to listen and obey], tell it to the church; and if he refuses to listen even to the church, let him be to you as a pagan and a tax collector." (AMP)

Matthew 5:23-24
"Therefore, if you are offering your gift at the altar and there remember that your brother has something against you, leave your gift there in front of the altar. First go and be reconciled to your brother; then come and offer your gift."

Matthew 18:35

"This is how my heavenly Father will treat each of you unless you forgive your brother from your heart."

"So also My heavenly Father will deal with every one of you if you do not freely forgive your brother from your heart his offenses." (AMP)

Matthew 18:21-22

"Then Peter came to Jesus and asked, 'Lord, how many times shall I forgive my brother when he sins against me? Up to seven times?' Jesus answered, 'I tell you, not seven times, but seventy-seven times.'"

"Then Peter came up to Him and said, 'Lord, how many times may my brother sin against me and I forgive him and let it go? [As many as] up to seven times?' Jesus answered him, 'I tell you, not up to seven times, but seventy times seven!'" (AMP)

Luke 17:3-4

"If your brother sins, rebuke him, and if he repents, forgive him. If he sins against you seven times in a day and seven times comes back to you and says, 'I repent,' forgive him."

"If your brother sins (misses the mark), solemnly tell him so and reprove him, and if he repents (feels sorry for having sinned), forgive him. And even if he sins against you seven times in a day, and turns to you seven times and says, I repent [I am sorry] you must forgive him (give up resentment and consider the offense as recalled and annulled)." (AMP)

I Corinthians 13:5

Love "keeps no record of wrongs."

Luke 23:34
"Father forgive them for they do not know what they are doing."

Asking God for Forgiveness
(emphases mine)

I John 1:9
"If we confess our sins, he is faithful and just and will forgive us our sins and purify us from *all* unrighteousness."

"If we [freely] admit that we have sinned and confess our sins, He is faithful and just (true to His own nature and promises) and will forgive our sins [dismiss our lawlessness] and *[continuously] cleanse us* from *all* unrighteousness [everything not in conformity to His will in purpose, thought, and action]." (AMP)

Isaiah 43:25
"I, even I, am He who blots out your transgressions, *for my own sake*, and remembers your sins no more."

2 Peter 3:9
"The Lord is not slow in keeping his promise, as some understand slowness. He is patient with you, not wanting anyone to perish, but everyone to come to repentance."

Psalm 51: 1-12, 17
"Have mercy on me, O God according to your unfailing love; according to your great compassion blot out my transgressions. Wash away all my iniquity and cleanse me from my sin.

For I know my transgressions and my sin in always before me. Against you, you only, have I sinned and done what is evil in your sight, so that you are proved right when you speak and justified when you judge. Surely I was sinful at birth, sinful from the time my mother conceived me. Surely you desire truth in the inner parts; you teach me wisdom in the inmost place.

Cleanse me with hyssop, and I will be clean; wash me, and I will be whiter than snow. Let me hear joy and gladness; let the bones you have crushed rejoice. Hide your face from my sins and blot out all my iniquity.

Create in me a pure heart, O God, and renew a steadfast spirit within me. Do not cast me from your presence or take your Holy Spirit from me. Restore to me the joy of your salvation and grant me willing spirit, to sustain me....

The sacrifices of God are a broken spirit; a broken and contrite heart you will not despise."

Forgiving Yourself

Matthew 23:39
"Love your neighbor as yourself."

Romans 8:1-2
"Therefore, *there is now no condemnation* for those who are in Christ Jesus, because through Christ Jesus the law of the Spirit of life set me free from the law of sin and death."

Appendix Two:
About the Contributing Authors

Gwen Ebner

Gwen Ebner is a professor at Winebrenner Seminary. She has published three books and one article. She also has a website, www.PersonalGrowthForMe.com that reflects her passion for helping others grow in a holistic way.

Renee Johnson Fisher

Renee Johnson Fisher is a spirited speaker and writer to twenty-somethings. She graduated from Biola University and worked with nationally known Christian speakers and writers at Outreach Events. She is the author of Faithbook of Jesus and Not Another Dating Book. She and her husband Marc live in Escondido, CA where they hope to adopt a *big* dog soon. www.DevotionalDiva.com

Janet Perez Eckles

Although blind, Janet Perez Eckles has been inspiring thousands to see the best in life. Her journey from trials to triumph appear in more than 28 anthologies, and in her own releases including #1 bestselling, *Simply Salsa: Dancing without Fear at God's Fiesta, Judson Press, 2011.* www.janetperezeckles.com

Carlynn

Carlynn is a retired RN, a dog trainer, a wildlife habitat creator, and a minimalist who loves the outdoors. It is there, in the midst of nature, that she best hears God's voice. She sees God in the creeks and waterfalls, the mountains and meadows, and in the serendipitous wildflowers growing all over Creation. Mercy for a Murderer is an excerpt from Carlynn's book *Angels in the Landfill (Mixed Blessings and Saving Graces)*, which will soon be out in e-reader version. She writes only by her first name because, as she says, "it isn't about me; it's *all* about God."

Yvonne Pat Wright

Yvonne Pat Wright., an author, speaker and lay preacher. After years of working in evangelism her first book" From Spice to Eternity: Discovering the main Ingredient to a Life of Fulfillment and Purpose is her attempt to share the gospel in a practical meaningful way. The book can be found on Amazon.com and more details at:
http://www.Spicetoeternity.co.uk

Saundra Dalton-Smith

Saundra Dalton-Smith is a physician, teacher, wife, and mother who is passionate about helping women overcome the mental barriers that prevent them from living free in Christ. She combines the knowledge and compassion of her medical training with biblical principles to offer those bound by insecurity, anxiety, fear, and doubt her prescription for living free. She is the author of Set Free to Live Free: Breaking

Through the 7 Lies Women Tell Themselves. To learn more about Saundra visit <u>www.setfreetolivefreebook.com</u>

RaeLynn DeAngelis

Author, speaker and ministry leader, Rae Lynn DeAngelis, is passionate to share the power of God's Word in her life. Her book, *Nothing But Your Truth Will Help Me, God*, tells of her spiritual journey to freedom after suffering with the eating disorder, bulimia, for twenty-five years. In 2008, Rae Lynn started a non-profit organization called, *Living in Truth Ministries,* which helps women break free from strongholds through the truth of God's Word. (John 8:32) <u>www.livingintruthministries.com</u>

Antonia Faisant

Antonia Faisant is a wife and stay at home mother of two children. She is active within her community and is in constant pursuit of a wonderful savior as she seeks and serves Him.

Elaine Marie Cooper

Elaine Marie Cooper is the author of the Deer Run Saga: *The Road to Deer Run* (2010), *The Promise of Deer Run* (2011), and *The Legacy of Deer Run* (due in 2012). She is also a contributing writer for *Fighting Fear: Winning the War at Home* by Edie Melson.

Heather Hart

Co-author and editor of *"Teen Devotions... for Girls!"*, Heather is a servant of Christ, whose desire is to grow more like Jesus each day. She enjoys sharing her faith with others through writing and strives to please Christ in all she does (Gal. 1:10). Heather and her husband Paul live in Colorado, where she fills her days caring for their four young children, writing for Christ, and studying God's Word. You can find Heather writing online at ServantWifeMother.blogspot.com

Chuck Sandstrom

Dr. Chuck Sandstrom was the victim of a random, violent assault in June of 2009 and, though still physically and cognitively impaired, continues to inspire audiences with powerful messages drawn from his personal story of recovery and forgiveness, a story that has been closely followed by the Akron Beacon Journal. You can find out more about Chuck and his wife Auburn at www.ChuckSandstrom.org

Patty Mason

Patty Mason is a wife and mother who found hope and healing when Jesus reached into her well of depression and set her free. From her painful past God created Liberty in Christ Ministries, a ministry dedicated to helping others find hope, healing, and freedom for their souls. As a speaker and Bible teacher, Patty has reached audiences all over the world through Sisters on Assignment, Christian TV, Sermon.net, Salem Communication's Light Source, and WLGT Blog Radio Live. Most recently, her story was featured on CBN, 700 Club.

Her books include, *Transformed by Desire: A Journey of Awakening to Life and Love,* and *Finally Free: Breaking the Bonds of Depression Without Drugs.* For more information visit: www.libertyinchristministries.net

Rita

All honor, glory, and praise to Him for allowing me to be able to write down and share my personal thoughts and feelings. While what is and has been important to me in my life, may not be fully understood by others, being given the opportunity to express myself in the written form helps in my healing. In order to forgive someone else, you have to forgive yourself first - it should always start from within. Thank you, CJ and Shelley for allowing me to share my healing!

S'ambrosia Curtis

S'ambrosia Curtis is the Online Ministry Coordinator for the Find Your True Beauty website and a middle school and high school English teacher at Salina Christian Academy.

Tom Blubaugh

Tom Blubaugh is a freelance writer living in Southwest Missouri with Barbara, his wife. Tom has written non-fiction most of his adult life, but has recently written a historical fiction titled *Night of the Cossack*, published by Bound by Faith Publishers.
http://tomblubaugh.com

Nathan Buck

Nathan Buck is the founding pastor of The Catalyst Church, in Findlay, OH. He is an active Potter's Apprentice, with a hobby business called Yatzar Earthenware, and a speaker for Worldview Warriors. His passion is to help people dig deep into God's Word, and he enjoys finding artistic and creative ways to join in God's mission to bring others into relationship with Himself. Nate treasures the support and partnership of his beloved wife Alison, and their three children. His other interests often include: singing, songwriting, acting, disc golf, exercising, and coffee.

Christina Ryan Claypool

Christina Ryan Claypool is a dynamic speaker and author of the book, *"Forgiven finding peace in the aftermath of abortion,"* which has been endorsed by Dr. John Willke. Her latest book, *Seeds of Hope for Survivors* is a tool for healing the victimized, addicted, or brokenhearted.

She has been featured on CBN's 700 Club and on Joyce Meyer Ministries *Enjoying Everyday Life.* Contact her through her Website at www.christinaryanclaypool.com

Julie Lambie

Julie Lambie is married and lives in Nsw Australia. Julie lives on 28 acres and is passionate about reading writing and worship. Julie has raised 6 children and is raising her 8 yr old grandchild after the loss of her eldest daughter.

Scott Mason

Overall, Scott was committed to 2 psychiatric hospitals, arrested over 25 times (2 times by S.W.A.T.) appeared before 15 judges in 12 courts, tried and convicted of 36 felonies, spent 10 years in 16 prisons where he became a ranking gang member for a powerful prison gang. One night while attending an event in a prison chapel Scott's life was forever changed. In this graphic personal story, Scott tells of a time where drugs, alcohol, sex, attempted suicide, crime and prison ruled his life, and how two men one who hung on a cross for him and the other doing life in prison completely changed his life. www.ScottMason.org

Kimberley Payne

Kimberley Payne is a motivational speaker and author. Her writings relate raising a family, pursuing a healthy lifestyle, and everyday experiences to building a relationship with God. Through her work, Kimberley hopes to inspire people to live their life to glorify God. You can visit her website at www.kimberleypayne.com

LaToya Gay

LaToya Gay is a 28 year wife and mother to a God-fearing man and blessed with three beautiful children. LaToya has a passion for helping other young women realize their true worth and showing them that they can two go through the healing process through forgiveness, prayer, and staying in the word. Through her hurt and pain it took her almost 28 years to realize that all of the emotions and anger that she had been bottling up inside was taking a toll on her physical as well as spiritual health.. With being said, she refuses to allow anyone to go through life harboring unforgiveness in their hearts and allowing their fears and past torture them endlessly because of what they do not know.. It is time to release and LaToya has challenged herself to help those who need healing.

Michael Okyere Asante

Michael Okyere Asante is a devotional writer, Christian blogger, author, and basic school teacher. Through his writings he calls Christians to draw closer to God, and lukewarm and backsliding Christians to return to their first love. He writes for the "NUPS-G Observer", a publication of the National Union of Presbyterian Students-Ghana, and blogs generally on the Christian life at:

http://michaelasante.blog.com

CJ and Shelley Hitz

CJ and Shelley Hitz have co-authored the best-selling book *"Forgiveness Formula: Finding Lasting Freedom in Christ."* They enjoy sharing God's Truth through their speaking engagements and their writing. On downtime, they enjoy spending time outdoors running, hiking and exploring God's beautiful creation. You can find out more about their ministry at www.TheForgivenessFormula.com

CJ and Shelley's Contact Information:

We would love to hear from you! Also, send your prayer requests, so that we can specifically pray for you.
Send us an e-mail or a letter to the following address:

cj@cjhitz.com
shelley@shelleyhitz.com

P.O. Box 1757
Findlay, Ohio 45839
1-800-230-4390

Websites:

www.TheForgivenessFormula.com
www.ChristianSpeakers.tv
www.FindYourTrueBeauty.com

Read CJ and Shelley's Other Best-Selling Books:

Forgiveness Formula: Finding Lasting Freedom in Christ by CJ and Shelley Hitz

Fuel for the Soul: 21 Devotionals that Nourish by CJ Hitz

Mirror Mirror...Am I Beautiful? Looking Deeper to Find Your True Beauty by Shelley Hitz

Teen Devotionals...for Girls! By Shelley Hitz and Heather Hart

The Edge Books

He said to her, "Woman, where are those accusers of yours? Has no one condemned you?" She said, "No one, Lord." And Jesus said to her, "Neither do I condemn you; go and sin no more." Then Jesus spoke to them again, saying, "I am the light of the world. He who follows Me shall not walk in darkness, but have the light of life." (Jn 8:10-11 NKJ)

Find Out More:

On Twitter https://twitter.com/TheEdge_Books

Website www.TheEdgeBooks.blogspot.com

On Facebook www.facebook.com/TheEdgeBooks

And Pinterest www.pinterest.com/lmarshall41/the-edge